MENDING
THE WEST

SIMON LENNON

Mending the West
Non-Fiction (Social Sciences, Philosophy)
A book in the collection: The West
Published by Pine Hill Books
Copyright © 2025 by Simon Lennon.
All rights reserved.
ISBN 978-1-925446-46-3 (electronic)
ISBN 978-1-925446-47-0 (paperback)
59,000 words, including the preface
Cover image: Three of the author's children at Bundanoon, 2015

CONTENTS

PREFACE

School did not teach me to question. Neither did my first three university degrees.

My fourth degree was a Master of Business Administration from Macquarie University. The course Foundations of Management Thought introduced me to philosophy.

A decade later, early in 2004, ideas began gestating in my mind. Writing from late 2006 let my thoughts progress. Words should provoke thought.

My collection of non-fiction books *The West* originated in my corporate legal experiences. A point made in that philosophy course was that corporations reflect the countries outside. Thus seeking to understand Western corporations is seeking to understand the West, and how we came to be like this.

Commencing with *Western Individualism*, my first series of three books I had envisaged becoming a doctoral thesis, until I discovered the pointlessness of doctoral theses. The remaining eight books of the initial eleven were essentially appendices to that first series, organised into three more series: identity, nationalism, and cultures.

Summarising each of the four series were my four ensuing overview books. They collated ideas without the facts behind them, along with ideas to which those ideas led and more facts for good measure.

The more I thought, the more I wrote. The more I wrote, the further my thoughts.

Until the Great War, many of those thoughts and ideas were self-evident. They have become increasingly controversial, even offensive, in the West since then, especially since the Holocaust. They remain self-evident to most of the world.

Understanding the causes and conflicts that brought the West to the extraordinary state in which we now lie might be enough for people indifferent to us. It is not enough for people who care. The value of understanding is in recovery.

This final book in the collection responds to the preceding books. It is the book for progression.

I could not have written this book without having written the first eleven books, collecting evidence and developing ideas, and then the four overview books, collating and elaborating upon those ideas. I could not have written any of these books without having studied Western philosophy in that single university course in 1993.

White people remain extraordinarily uninterested in what other races think, feel, and do, but we should not ignore them remaining as we too used to be. We should not excuse them, for there is nothing to excuse. Instead of mindlessly lauding other races, we should emulate them, regarding matters of human nature. We need to be less unique.

To learn, we need information. If we are not allowed to tell stories of people from other races but must submit to them telling us their stories, then that leaves us only with stories from our race to tell.

Every ethnicity outside the West looks at the world and events from its perspective. We should do so from ours.

The voices we men, women, and children need to hear are those of our own, especially our poor, elderly, and other most vulnerable. Without our fickle wealth and passing youth, we are they.

We need to hear the voices of our ancestors and descendants, especially our forebears who worked, fought, and died for us. But for time, we are they. We are descendants of the long dead and ancestors of the unborn.

When the Great War ended in 1918, we knew we were broken because before the war began, we were whole. When relief and celebration for the end of World War II had passed, we felt gutted because we remembered feeling something inside us before that war began, in 1939.

America's optimism in the 1950s was technological, in a land spared the death and ruin in Europe, but Europeans and colonial Europeans alike lost our sense of being peoples. We lost our roots.

What we did not lose of ourselves and our cultures through those first decades after World War II, we stopped passing to our next generation. Parents believed but did not believe enough to practice or to teach their children. Their children becoming teenagers lost their connectedness with their parents to ask.

Schools ceased feeling that their traditional ethnicities' histories and cultures were their role to teach. Writers and film-makers looked elsewhere for inspiration.

Our hearts through the years became empty, while we remembered less and less of what our hearts felt to be full. We lost our souls.

We lost our confidence in natural order. We lost our sense there

1. HUMANNESS

We of the West might presume we are normal. We used to be.

Alternatively, we might assume there are no normalities in people's feelings, beliefs, and behaviours. There are.

We have become unique in the world. We have become unique through history.

People knowing we are unique might think we are uniquely bad. We are not.

Along with our friends, we might presume we are personally progressive. As the rest of the world knows, we are not.

Understanding cultures and civilisations requires observing not just the world but the people around it, now and through history. Other races but ours remain normal, albeit with racial differences.

Mentally and emotionally, we have deteriorated since 1914, the start of the Great War. We have deteriorated most markedly since 1945, the end of World War II.

Our deterioration has accelerated over time, exacerbated by each preceding phase of our deterioration. By any measure of the earth and eternity, we have become increasingly abnormal, unnatural, and irrational. When the abnormal, unnatural, and irrational become routine, they can seem normal, natural, and rational, to people knowing nothing else.

Abnormality, unnaturalness, and irrationality are generally symptomatic of something wrong, or at least of something less than ideal, in people and populations. Something is wrong with the West.

"The West is in relative decline," New South Wales senator Devanand Sharma, an Indian, warned a dinner at the Killara Golf Club in November 2025. "It is not in terminal decline."

Everything to say of the West, we can say of most Western countries. The timing and details vary between countries and between regions and areas within countries, but the themes and trends are largely the same. What we say of races and ethnicities, we can say of families within those races and ethnicities.

was natural order. People not feeling broken or not knowing they are broken can still be broken, when being broken is all they know.

Western brokenness is Western post-nationalist individualism. You are just you, I am just I, and he or she is just he or she, without reference to a broader people like family, race, or collective religion.

Other races still feel what we no longer feel. They retain their roots and connectedness: their ethnicities. They thus retain their countries and cultures. Most prosper.

A century after the Great War, we have not yet recovered. We try to fill our emptiness with other races' roots and cultures, but know they are not ours. We presume to know peace, but do not know peace of mind. We might talk of humanity and being human, but without contemplating what being human means. We do not know human fulfilment, or how humanness feels. Ill at ease with ourselves, human nature eludes us.

Human nature is flawed. It is human nature nevertheless.

Humanness includes the mental, emotional, and thus behavioural. Denying us our humanness or other races their humanness is ideological.

From our human nature come certain instincts. People not feeling those instincts in the unnatural circumstances of their lives does not mean those instincts are not there.

If we noticed people amidst the numbers then we would see that much of the economies we call ours and are so keen to grow are not our economies. Other races' businesses in our names, countries, and histories are still other races' businesses. Their wealth is theirs, not ours.

Many Western ethnicities' economies are declining. They have been for years. We are declining.

To accept ourselves dying while the economies continue is to accept ourselves dying. Frightened as we have become of our shadows, we are ambivalent to our collective existence.

Were a loved one so deeply scarred by distress as two world wars, especially the Jewish Holocaust during World War II, scar the West, we would want her to heal. Were a loved one self-destructively stupid as the West has become, we would want him to turn his life around. Healing the West heals us individually too.

Mending the West requires us to recognise what broke us. Healing our ethnicities requires us to recognise what gutted us.

Saving our families requires us to recognise what erases us.

Ideologies are not erasing us. They only matter if people believe them, or behave as if they believe them.

The weather is not erasing us. We need not fear climate or nature. We are nature.

A virus or vaccine is not erasing us. Other races and their religions are not erasing us.

People harming us do so because we permit them. Anything erasing us does so because we allow it. We invite it.

We broke us. We gutted us. We are erasing us.

Perhaps never before in history has a people's greatest enemy been within, not just within a people's countries but within a people's minds. Ours now is.

Inviting our collective decline and fall is irrational, but we need to correct the causes of our decline if we are to correct our decline. To want to survive, we need to know we exist. We need to know that we matter.

Our souls remain ours to sense again. Only we can start to fill the emptiness inside us.

The so-called culture wars around the West are people valuing themselves and their cultures more than they value other people's money. Recognising the richness that being human can be, we might find fulfilment in family, friendships, and community. We might reason enough to question at least some ideology, wanting to inspire others to question too. Cherishing nature, we might dare to think, feel, and act naturally.

In unnatural environments come unnatural ideas, desires, and behaviours. Ideologies have become unnatural, however natural their objectives. Individualism is unnatural.

Ideologies of inclusion and diversity commoditise people, reducing them to their economic or political uses. Some of us focus upon money. Others of us focus upon ideology, provided the people focused upon money concur.

Instead of seeing buyers and sellers, workers and spenders, voters and victims, we need again to see people: us and everyone else. Human beings are more than mere political and economic units: factors in commercial production and consumption, fodder for our ideological drives. People have interests beyond those measured by monetary transactions or by our perceptions of them and of us.

worthwhile.

Worthwhile activities improve at least one person's health, happiness, or security. The improvement need not be much. It needs to be something.

Fine arts bring pleasure, long after the labour to make them is done; our cultural and other heritages await us. Dances, rituals, and other aspects of amateur culture need not be labour at all.

Fresh air and clear water can invigorate us. The sight of sky by day or by night can delight us. The stars across heaven, craters of the moon, and creases in a green leaf can intrigue us. Birds, animals, and fish can enthral us.

Our betterment can be safety and sanctuary. It can be love and relationship.

A man's hug or holding of hands can comfort a woman far more than anything she buys. The touch of a woman can thrill a man far more than anything for sale. Those friendships can beguile us.

Our children can charm us. Contemplating our ancestors can console us.

None of these likings needs to involve economic activity, even if it happens they do. Money can be a poor measure of the pleasures they provide.

We have come to idealise primitive peoples for traits that used to be ours, enjoying simple pleasures like resting by a stream. Pastimes used to be largely universal, remaining ours until recently, especially in our childhoods. In the 1970s, my school friends and I caught yabbies in a creek.

At some point, we need to stop simply lauding primitive races for retaining their primitive natures. We need to recognise every race's primitive nature, especially ours.

To know human fulfilment, we need to recall what being human means. We need to remember how humanness feels.

Western authorities no longer affirm human nature. They suppress, deny, or distract us from our natures.

Human authorities might be governments, bureaucracies, or big businesses. They might be news media, advertisers, or the makers of films and television programmes. They might be courts, the police, or anything else human presiding over people, in practice or law. They might be schools or universities, or parents letting others dictate their parenting.

Those authorities might initially have had the best of intentions. They might still have the best of intentions.

Ultimately, we remain like other races, because neither we nor anyone else can change human nature. We can only lose sense of it.

Human nature remains within us to recover. We need to reach beyond influences we have let corrupt us. We need to free ourselves from distractions.

Nothing needs to go back into a box. We need to come out of ours.

Reality and reason reveal nature and normalcy. To know what wishes, values, and lifestyles are natural, we can begin with those that were traditional. They became traditions because they were natural.

Individually, we are not as intrinsically unique as we think we are. To recognise the commonalities in human feelings, beliefs, and behaviours across the world and through history, as we do to deny racial differences, is to acknowledge human nature.

Tempering our observations is recognition of our worsening Western waywardness since World War I, and especially since World War II. They are reasons to put aside the strange recent West, in articulating what actions, moods, and desires make up human nature. If people feeling enlightened with their ideologies knew of the world and of history, they would realise how perverse the West has become.

The rest of the world and human history are in many respects uniform. That uniformity points to human nature.

There are racial commonalities in human nature. There are racial differences. Both are important.

Often, human nature is simply nature, common between humans and animals. There is a natural world of which we are part. We always were.

Our needs are to feel grass or soil underfoot and to smell leaves and flowers nearby. They are to sense our natural selves within us, without dwelling upon individual us.

Any sustainable lifestyle respects human nature. So much of saving a suicidal family and ethnicity is simply living again by human nature.

All we need want is what other races still want, as we used to want. All we need do is again what other races still do.

Acknowledging the implications and consequences of being

human invites us to experience, enjoy, and celebrate our natural instincts and desires. There is only nature and not.

We lost sight of it through the twentieth century, but being human can be delightful. Human fulfilment is unlikely to lie in humans being anything else.

2. REALITY

Two types of people equate their truth with other people's truths, as if each person has his or her truth and there is no absolute truth. One type is philosophers, although only some philosophers. The other type is liars. There are very few philosophers left in the world.

Postmodernism varies and encompasses much, but its most telling frequent feature is relativism: the rejection of objective reality in favour of each person's subjective reality. Philosophically the idea is old, but it never before mattered as it came to matter through the twentieth-century West.

Moral, religious, and philosophical conviction in objective reality declined. Morality, Christianity, and philosophy declined.

Community, society, and civilisation are all predicated upon people co-operating with each other, at least to some degree. If each person has a personal reality, how can people co-operate? How can people connect? Relativism is individualism: the end of society and civilisation, without anybody noticing.

There is no personal reality. It does not exist.

The only reality is objective. If reality is not objective, then it is not reality.

People need at least some structure in their lives, if only to get the food and water they need to eat and drink. Societies and civilisations require structure, or they are not societies and civilisations.

Structure does not need to be tangible, but it needs to be real, not imagined. Reality is the foundation of structure.

Reality is not narrow. It is not extremism.

Reality is truth. It is the starting point for all other truth.

A commitment to truth seeks knowledge of reality. Reality exists.

If we do not start with reality, with facts, then logic and science cannot teach us anything. Reason and the scientific method begin with reality, however frustrating, irritating, or painful the reality.

Through the first half of the twentieth century, reality became painful. Thus the West began separating from reality regarding our most important of knowledge: that about people.

The West remains for the most part engaged with reality in fields such as physics, engineering, and technology. They are not the fields in which we are failing.

Theoretically, relativism means people believe what they wish. They say what they like. If it feels true then it is true, however untrue it is.

In practice, relativism means more than people dismissing reality as simply one person's truth, of no interest to anyone. Without reality constraining them, human authorities decree the truth. They decree reality.

People say what authorities and soon enough other people want to hear. They succumb.

Reacquainting ourselves with reality requires us to recognise this era for what it is: our Age of Ideology. Originating in 1796 in our Age of Enlightenment, French philosopher Antoine Destutt de Tracy devised ideology as the science of ideas.

De Tracy sought a cohesive structure of rational ideas grounded in classical liberalism. Ideologies began with idealism.

France's leader from 1799, Napoleon Bonaparte dismissed as dreamers what he called the ideologues. Ideology ceased being the science. Ideologies became the suites of ideas.

Napoleon consolidated power with himself, essentially implementing an ideology later called Bonapartism. Ideologies remained engaged with reality, but were no longer necessarily liberal.

Ideologies are premised upon the appeal of the ideology, especially for people needing that appeal. Following our two world wars and the worsening breakdown of our families and communities thereafter, we have increasingly needed that appeal.

An ideology might not intend to disregard reality, but the rigour in which people hold it makes it impervious to reality. Ideology became the imposition of an idea or suite of ideas without regard for the facts.

It might denote something true that is demonstrably untrue. It might denote something untrue that is demonstrably true. It might denote something true or untrue for which there is no evidence either way.

Being false does not make an idea or suite of ideas a relativist ideology, if it appears true or possibly true on the evidence. What begins as an idea becomes a post-truth ideology if fresh evidence proves the idea false but people persist with saying it is true, or the idea fails in practice but people persist with implementing it.

We persist. Reality became superfluous.

Central to ideologies has become declaring matters true or false not to reflect reality, but in furtherance of political, economic, or social purposes. Those purposes might be good purposes. They might not. They might suit some people at the expense of other people.

Thus ideologies have become much like the most vacuous and misleading of commercial marketing, but for the most prominent political purposes instead of minor monetary motives. To the extent that economics is politics or politics is economics, they are the same.

Saying something over and over does not make it true. Writing and rewriting does not change the facts. The louder and more often people feel compelled to say something, the less likely it is to be true.

Ideologies are not real. Our Age of Ideology is an Age of Unreality.

To recognise reality is to refuse to subscribe to ideologies. If ideology made reality obsolete, then returning to reality should make ideology obsolete.

Ideas could remain simply ideas, beholden to reality. Ideologies could again be suites of ideas all beholden to reality, as their proponents claim them to be.

Through the twentieth century, critics of ideology sometimes incorporated in their definitions of ideology a lack of regard for the impact of those ideas upon people, but to disregard reality is to disregard the consequences of reality upon people. The reality that ideologies have come to disregard includes human nature.

To know reality, we need clarity in the words we speak, hear, write, and read. We need clarity in our thoughts.

The only useful definitions are those that allow people to communicate clearly with others and to think lucidly inside their heads. If communications are not clear, they are not communications. If thoughts are not lucid, people are confused, perhaps even crazy.

Ideologies are words, often dependent upon redefining words. Ideological redefinitions seek not to communicate, but to change the way people think and feel. They defy human nature.

Redefining words can make any falsehood true. When anything can be true, with suitable definition, then truth becomes meaningless.

Language needs to convey information and that information needs to be true. Words should describe accurately what they purport to describe. Definitions should defer to reality.

However well-intentioned ideologies might appear to be in theory, without grounding in reality, they can do no good in reality. Relativism condemns people to ignorance, error, and often harm.

Reality at any instant is definitive, even if our particular perspectives and understandings of reality are not. Relativism is a failure to distinguish knowledge and perception from reality. Ideology became the same.

Engaging with reality requires rejecting relativism. Reality is absolute.

People insisting their beliefs or perceptions amount to reality, whatever the facts, are arrogant. They adopt God's role.

Reality does not depend upon laws or public opinion: what people say, think, or feel. Reality does not depend upon people knowing it.

A fact remains a fact even if nobody believes it. A falsehood does not become a fact even if everyone believes it, however zealously everyone does.

Facts and reason alone cannot easily counter ideology that facts and reason did not produce. Overcoming falsities arising from feelings must appeal to feelings: to the comfort of reality and joy of reason.

Feelings can be wonderful, but should complement, not supersede, facts and reason. Feelings never warrant rejecting facts or reason. Even doubt should be reasonable.

Feelings can also be burdensome. Facts, reason, and response might alleviate that burden.

Facts are generally simple, even if discovering them and understanding them are not. Structure needs simplicity.

Without reality to ground them, ideologies are often complicated, trying to satisfy multiple purposes. They can create confusion and ambiguity where there should be certainty and clarity.

Ideas, however meritorious or not, reside in people's minds. Thoughts, values, and opinions are transient. Ideas change.

Some ideologies become abnormal norms or untrue truisms. Others fleet in and fleet out.

Year upon year, new ideologies unfold. Fashion is no longer simply clothes, hair, and occasionally yo-yos and hula-hoops. It includes every ideological fad. Keeping up can be difficult.

Compounding upon established ideologies, ideologies become more and more absurd, although none more obviously absurd than the last. Once people disengage from reality, there is no logical limit to lying.

Lying is bad enough. Foisting a falsehood upon others is worse. Compelling people to lie is oppression.

Ideologues and ideologies' purveyors might presume their purposes make them right, but their economic, political, and other interests are often individual, sectional, or alien to people upon whom they impose their ideologies. Their righteousness is thus also individual, sectional, or alien. It is not a collective righteousness born of a common good.

People imposing their sense of righteousness upon others not sharing their interests are either arrogant or malevolent. Their ideologies are either arrogant or malevolent.

We need to lose our arrogance. If our arrogance was warranted, we would not be in decline.

Falling afoul of reality, ideologies are ultimately delusions or lies. Reality might not be pretty, but reality has implications we should know, even if we then disregard those implications. However sweet the ideology, we all have to live in reality.

Discarding reality is escapism. It is lying.

There are people who think that lies and other falsehoods point to truths, but lies and falsehoods never point to truths. They can only point to more lies and falsehoods.

Truth is based upon fact. Any purported truth that falls foul of the facts is not truth. It might be an error, a lie, or ideology.

Subject to that caveat, creative fiction is not lying. It is imagination, not pretending to be fact.

Fiction only means something in contrast with non-fiction. Without recognition of reality there is no imagination.

Writers, film-makers, and other artists need not always depict reality, but they should not falsify reality. Works of fiction must present the world honestly. When works portray fantasy worlds, inferences they make of reality should be truthful.

Fiction can reveal truths. Lies cannot.

To know reality, we must want to know. We need to cease tolerating lies, be those lies ours or anyone else's.

Facts are not smart or stupid. People are smart or stupid.

Why would anyone want the right to be wrong? Erring is unfortunate and inadvertent error or inescapable ignorance not a fault, but wilful ignorance or error is a fault, when the means to knowledge is at hand.

Facts are facts whoever says them. Falsehoods are false whoever decrees them.

Reality does not depend upon who pays to discover or report it. Reality does not depend upon who benefits by it, although reality as it becomes in the future might so depend.

Without a commitment to truth, reporting what purports to be reality does depend upon who pays and who benefits. So does ideology.

Commitments to reality teach reality to others, but we need to know the truth to tell the truth. We should read and listen to words of people who write and talk of reality.

Traditional journalist ethics sought knowledge of reality to then impart that knowledge to others. Journalists reported facts as they were, or possibly will be.

They reported allegations as allegations; the law demands it of allegations in court. Where there were two sides to a story, journalists presented both sides. They reported claims and counterclaims for readers and listeners to form their views. Audiences, not journalists, decided what pertained.

To learn later that something reported was untrue embarrassed journalists and newspapers of record. The immediate remedy was retraction, correction, and apology.

If authorities want to be trusted, they need to be trustworthy. They need to be truthful.

We cannot rely upon any person or authority whose aim is anything but the truth, as best as he, she, or it can determine. That can be difficult to discern.

From where knowledge comes matters less than does the knowledge itself. We are more likely to learn the truth from a plurality of sources than from a single source.

Some people want to read and hear facts. Other people do not. They tend to be different facts for different people.

Reality is all reality come what may, or it might not be reality. Bits of reality can misrepresent reality.

Dismissing inconvenient facts by labelling them irrelevant does not make them any less factual. Nor does it make them any less relevant. That facts are inconvenient probably means they are particularly relevant.

Facts that do not suit our point of view are not misinformation. They are facts. Misinformation presents as fact information not factual.

There might be alternative arguments, drawn from alternative streams of evidence, or even the same stream of evidence. There are no alternative facts. There are only facts.

If the purported fact is not a fact, the counter is evidence that it is not a fact. That is debate.

The only counters to facts are more facts. That too is debate.

Theories, opinion, and advocacy come after we are apprised of the facts. If facts undermine our theory or opinion, then we should amend our theory or opinion. If our advocacy does not accord with reality, then we should cease advocating.

We need to be willing to hear, read, and believe facts challenging beliefs we hold dear. Facts might corroborate our suspicions or refute our passionately held beliefs, about matters of the greatest importance, but they are still simply facts.

Being unpalatable does not make facts any less factual. Unpalatable facts should make us question what we find palatable, and the reasons we do.

Some people imagine lies and falsehoods achieving worthwhile purposes. Putting aside the most extraordinary moments of risk and conflict, no worthwhile purpose depends upon us misleading our compatriots.

Denying there is a problem does not solve the problem. Prohibiting talk of reality does not prohibit reality. Facts remain unsaid, but remain.

Labelling unfounded claims and untruths as being facts does not make them true. It does not make them facts.

Falsifying reality does not change reality. People and authorities can lie and lie and lie again, leading other people to echo their lies, but no feeling, lie, or delusion of itself alters reality. No dream or desire, however noble and good, of itself alters anything.

Absolving people from facing their problems within them and before them, secrets and lies might help them feel better, but their problems remain. How can we deal with the difficulties of life if we do not admit those difficulties? How do we face the challenges of the world if we do not acknowledge those challenges?

There is normally no love in lying. If reality constrains us, then we need to be constrained.

Telling the truth does not create division. It exposes division already there.

Happiness and harmony that depend upon secrets and lies are not happiness or harmony. They are fraud. If fulfilling our political or social purposes depends upon secrets and lies, then we should question our purposes.

Holding populations together with secrets and lies does not avert conflict. To lie or otherwise deceive is conflict.

Lying and other deception are manipulation and oppression of the people deceived, however righteous or progressive the liars and deceivers presume their motivations to be. If people think that a fact is important enough for them to conceal it from their compatriots, then it is probably important enough for their compatriots to know.

Withholding information from our compatriots who could have used that information to take precautions protecting themselves or their families is immoral. Lies endangering our compatriots' health and safety are similarly immoral.

Problems fester and worsen, until the secrets and lies no longer hold. Falsehoods risk suffering and death.

Confronting reality is never more important than it is when reality is ugly. Only with knowledge of reality can we deal with reality, however awful that reality, however desperately we wish reality was otherwise.

Stating facts is not hatred. Telling an objective truth is not, of itself, harassment or abuse.

If revealing problems creates conflict then only the risk of conflict will prompt people to deal with those problems. If facts are inflammatory then we need to confront the reality by which facts have become inflammatory.

Words are not violence. They are words.

If the truth hurts, then we probably need to be hurt. If we find reality traumatising, then we probably need to be traumatised.

Conversely, reality frees us from false worries, letting us focus our minds and acts upon what matters. Reality matters.

How can we achieve anything without recognising reality? How can we enjoy the rewards of reality if we do not know what reality throws up?

People should have the right to be truthful, whatever the truth happens to be. We owe each other the facts, as best we know. If the truth is not everything, then it is nothing.

3. REASON

Some uniqueness we want. Through the late seventeenth, eighteenth, and early nineteenth centuries, Europe's Age of Enlightenment, our Age of Reason, centred the West with rational thought, the pursuit of happiness, and other ideals.

Engaging with reality is rational. Disregarding reality is irrational.

Reason is simple, straightforward deduction, drawing logical conclusions from assumptions. Those assumptions need to be rational: grounded in facts and evidence of facts. The existence of a single objective reality is a rational assumption.

Assumptions are merely assumptions. If a premise is false, then a logical conclusion drawn from that premise is probably false. No amount of reason applied to something that is true only because it is ideologically deemed to be true, without being in fact true, is likely to produce a hypothesis or conclusion that is in fact true.

Rational perceptions, analyses, and opinions are also grounded in fact and evidence of facts. They might prove to be right. They might prove to be wrong but point to what is right. They might simply be wrong.

To learn, we need to be willing to learn, reading and hearing all we can. Different analyses can teach us how little we know.

Interpretation and analysis are often subjective, but reason is ultimately objective, knowable by anyone rational. Reason is a matter of intellect.

We cannot know whether we are intelligent. We can only strive to be intelligent.

We need to think, not merely to be able to think. Thinking proves that we have minds: that we exist, even if we cannot prove that anyone else exists.

"I think, therefore I am," realised French philosopher René Descartes in the seventeenth century, underpinning classic Western liberalism. Underpinning our post-nationalist individualism is "I work, buy, or sell, therefore I am," or simply "I believe therefore I am," or "I feel therefore I am."

Among the Enlightenment ideals was scepticism. A rational analysis is a critical analysis.

Classic Western education taught critical analysis: the questioning of ideas, however popular those ideas. It considered conflicting ideas, however unpopular those ideas. Through debate, good ideas endured and foolish ideas withered. Students might agree or disagree.

Another Enlightenment ideal was individuality. To think is to think independently.

Thinking independently is to disregard fashion. It is neither to follow fashionable beliefs nor to gainsay them, purely for them being fashionable. We need not to trail mindlessly the loudest, nearest, or any other voices around.

Ideas and ideals can be rational or irrational. Rational ideals better us. If they better others, they do not harm us.

When ideology through the twentieth century became more important than reality, ideology also became more important than reason. Ideologies became intrinsically irrational when they became impervious to reality, however rational their origins or objectives.

Ideology replaced reality. Ideology replaced reason.

Conclusions replaced assumptions. Facts and logic became irrelevant.

Ideologies had always developed for political and social purposes, but they ceased developing through reason. They came to develop from feelings.

Our pursuit of happiness became patchy. It became narcissistic, momentary, and superficial.

We ceased bettering ourselves. We became willing to worsen ourselves.

Ideologies became anti-intellectual. Mental contortions trying to affirm irrational ideologies depend upon breaks in reason.

Irrational ideologies depend upon indoctrination, prohibiting knowledge of facts that disprove or might disprove the subjects of the indoctrination. Indoctrination excludes reason, suppressing independent thought, questioning, and critical analysis. It quashes competing and conflicting ideas. It forbids debate and dissent. It denies audiences a chance to escape.

Much of what we are told over and over is untrue. We hear untruths from people often unaware they speak untruthfully, or feeling unable to say they speak untruthfully.

Still, we should not instinctively assume everything we are told is untrue any more than we should believe everything we are told is true. We need only to question, without presuming the outcome of our questioning.

People telling anyone with whom they disagree to grow up presume that growing up means agreeing with them. It does not. Growing up in an age of reason means thinking independently.

Large numbers of people of all political colours blindly follow their political leaders, news services, and other human authorities. Their distinction is only that they might follow different authorities. They might follow the same authorities.

The claim that everyone believes something has become standard procedure for ideological propagandists, driving people to nonsense when there is no other means to persuade them. It starts as a lie but becomes self-fulfilling, among people unable or unwilling to think.

If the irrational can seem rational, then reason becomes unreliable. Ideologies imprison people's minds, producing intellectual wastelands of the topics they dictate. Our Age of Ideology devolved into an Age of Irrationality and Idiocy.

To end ideology is not just to engage with reality. It is to allow people freedom to think. That does not mean people will think, but they might.

Reason is not an ideology. Logic is logic irrespective of what anyone says.

Reason questions ideology. Reason questions everything.

Whatever authorities require of us, we have a tool to employ. Pressures and punishments compel people to say what they must to evade those pressures and punishments, so that lying becomes a matter of course, but they need not compel people to believe. We can think for ourselves.

Stepping back from hysteria is to stand apart from the mob. Close confidants grant us freedom to think and be truthful.

If we lack a circle of confidants, or even a single confidant, then we must think alone. If we cannot question aloud, then we must question in silence. We might sit in a chair or at a desk in our home, with a book or computer screen. We might walk through a forest or park, secretly recalling all we have read, seen, and heard.

We can begin by wondering what people mean by the words

and slogans they sprout. People routinely sprouting them might not know what they mean.

Words do not supersede facts. If the catchy slogans driving so much of the West are not untrue or irrational, even idiotic, they are normally meaningless. We should dispense with them.

Instead of trusting or not trusting what we read or hear because we trust or do not trust the writer or speaker, we can examine claims and ideas on their merits, from whenever and whomever they come. When we face claims and ideas apparently without merit, we might consider what we know that their proponents did not. We might consider what those proponents knew that we do not.

We might consider who had reason to espouse those claims and ideas, and whether their interests are ours. People's actions can be more telling than their words.

We might not know whether people are right or are wrong. Neither might they.

To reason is to wonder and ask. It is to question what we are told, even if the outcome of our questioning is to concur. We can question what people of our race say and what people of other races say.

Questioning claims with which we disagree is insufficient. We should question ideas with which we agree.

Asking people to question their beliefs, we must be willing to question ours. Asking them to amend or renounce their beliefs, we must be willing to amend or renounce ours, however long we have held our beliefs, perhaps for as long as we can recall. Mere belief is not evidence of truth.

Thus we must consider criticisms of our beliefs. Those criticisms might or might not be well-founded. We must think without the arrogance to insist our thoughts are always correct. Each thought might or might not be correct.

Reason is open to rational possibilities, including the possibility we are wrong. Reason does not keep people from being wrong. We learn we are wrong not because people declare us to be wrong, but because they teach us facts or reasoning by which we realise we are wrong.

If learning brings us to such realisation, honesty is to admit we were wrong: that even our most certain and fundamental belief was wrong. Admitting so should not be a burden. Learning we were wrong should be a relief, after having been wrong without realising it.

Realising our past errors might have all sorts of implications. It might have none. They are more matters for us to contemplate rationally.

If dialogue is not candid, it is not dialogue. Other races do not enjoy free speech and might not desire it, but they are not captive to ideologies as we have become.

Laws stifling free speech undermine people's respect for all laws and for governments enacting them. Pains and fears fester. Resentment worsens into hatred and anger, until laws no longer matter.

In our Age of Enlightenment, speech was free. In an Age of Re-Enlightenment, a Second Age of Reason, speech would again be free.

The only worthwhile equality is equality of opportunity, such as to speak. The only diversity of value is of viewpoint: thoughts and ideas. The most worthwhile inclusion is of people with whom we disagree.

Disagreement is not hatred. Reason is not hatred.

Free speech is not hate speech for challenging established ideas or for being provocative, venturing forth ideas for people to consider and discuss. Disagreement does not divide people unless they are already divided.

Rational people might disagree, debate, or dispute. They might feel disgusted, appalled, or repulsed. They do not ordinarily feel offended.

Offence is a feeling, increasingly of distress at encountering viewpoints with which people disagree or encountering facts countering their beliefs. A person's feelings are not reasons to deny other people their rights to speak or to hear. Feelings are personal.

If a person feels offended by our opinion, perception, or revelation, then we might wonder why the person feels offence. People's feelings might be reasons for us to moderate our behaviour, compose our words tactfully, or keep facts secret for a time.

They are not reasons to deny people knowledge forever, not even the people feeling offended. People's feelings are rarely, if ever, reasons to lie.

Our first question to answer should not be whether a feeling, opinion, or proposition is offensive. It should be whether a feeling is natural, an opinion rational, or a proposition true.

A proposition is not wrong because it offends people. Words offensive are often true. Prohibiting offence shuts down reason and reporting of reality.

Facts and reason are not offensive. They are facts and reason.

If facts and reason offend us, then we need to be offended. Offensive words might be the words that we most need to hear, to protect us and others for whom we care. We might suffer far more from being ignorant or wrong than we suffer feeling offended.

Feeling offence can be a claim to victimhood. It can be a claim to moral superiority.

It is not an intellectual process. It is not a rational argument.

Offence is unimportant, even to people offended, unless people make it important. Facts, reason, and contrary opinions do not offend rational people, unless they have an incentive to feel offended.

To let offence that some people feel shut down other people's free speech is to reward people for feeling offended. It encourages them to be even more self-absorbed: consumed by their feelings of offence rather than saying or doing anything worthwhile.

A right not to feel offended is a right to oppress. It is a right to force other people to silence and submission, dictating what they think, say, or do.

We have freedom to offend some people. If we truly believed in equality, people would be free to offend us. Free speech is free to offend.

Needing only to feel offence to silence anyone with whom we disagree does us no favours. Keeping us from having to argue our viewpoint denies us incentive to think through our viewpoint, forming our arguments.

It denies us the benefit of debate, hearing facts or reasoning that might correct or console us. Removing offence from consideration, people lazily feeling offended must adduce evidence and reason if they want to defend their views or persuade others.

If we cease kowtowing to people for fear of offending them, then they will be less likely to feel offended. Ignoring the people perpetually offended will lead them not to bother feeling offended or claiming to feel offended.

If powerful people were confident in their ideologies, they

would leave them as ideas. They would not enforce them. They would argue them. They would turn not to power or propaganda but to persuasion, with facts and reason. They would allow people to debate them.

People who refuse to debate presumably feel they cannot win those debates. If they refuse those debates because they presume that anyone with whom they disagree is a fool, they are arrogant in the extreme.

They are also wrong. People are not stupid because they disagree with us. They are not smart because they agree with us.

Intelligent people can be wrong. They can also be right.

Stupid people can be right. They can also be wrong.

Nor are people mentally ill because they disagree with us. They are not suffering a phobia.

Fears and concerns can be rational or irrational. Phobias are, by their traditional definition, irrational.

Thus only irrational fears are phobias. Rational fears and concerns do not become irrational because people call them phobias. Nor do morals.

Wise people do not presume anything about people with whom they disagree. They focus upon facts and evidence of facts. They look for logical reasoning and flaws.

If people are ignorant or wrong, then we ought to feel comfortable telling them the truth. If they are being irrational, then we should feel comfortable telling them what is rational.

People saying something untrue might be mistaken, lying, or irrational. Rational people mistaken in their assumptions, neglecting pertinent facts, or with reasoning flawed want to be critiqued. They want to be corrected.

They want someone to tell them the truth if they are ignorant or wrong. They want someone to tell them what is rational if they are being irrational. The two can then debate.

To persuade people rather than silence them, we need to understand them. We need to find the premises to their beliefs or steps in their thought processes with which we disagree. We need to listen.

Reason listens. By listening, we learn. By learning, we teach.

If we are certain of our position, debate is our chance to teach. Whether we are certain of our position, consumed by doubt, or something in between, debate is our chance not just to persuade but to learn.

We might be right, by which others can learn. We might be wrong, by which we can learn.

Debate compels people to think. Our thinking needs to be logical if we want others to be logical. Rational arguments convince rational people they are wrong.

We do not need to win debates. We need to have debates.

To lose a rational argument is good. It means we have learnt.

By learning, we win. There is no greater victory than to have been wrong but, through encountering new evidence or reasoning, to become right.

Debate teaches not only the debaters. It teaches the audience. Like judges and juries determining cases argued before them, audiences can adjudicate between alternative arguments.

Arguments ought to be substantiated with evidence. Aside from criminal prosecutions, to impose a greater burden of proof on one side than the other is not debate. It is intimidation.

Before a rational audience, persuasion is most likely to come from reason and courtesy. Paradoxically, being polite but irrational might prove more persuasive than being rude and rational.

Oratory and other rhetoric persuade. Among people devoted to reason, rhetoric seeks to be rational, although not everyone is devoted to reason. Good oratory without reason becomes more persuasive than poor oratory with reason.

That adds to the need for debate. Debate is the chance to critique even the finest of rhetoric, distinguishing the rational from the irrational.

Not only must we re-engage with reason and reality. We must insist others do too.

Debates do not dwell upon the debaters, but debate depends upon debaters being rational. Debate is never more difficult than it is with people making irrational assumptions or otherwise being irrational.

Trying to reason with the irrational would be irrational. The only point in listening to irrational people is trying to understand them.

Debating irrational people is debating alone. People cannot debate alone.

Without a shared devotion to reason, purported debates are at best conversations. They are at worst conflict.

Shouting is not debate. Drowning out dissent disallows debate.

Expletives are not argument. Profanities are not rhetoric. Abuse is not reason.

They are lazy, crass, and confrontational, indicative of people with nothing useful to say. They do not persuade people of anything, except to be quiet and look away.

4. THE SCIENTIFIC METHOD

Reason does not function in abstract, but in the context of reality. If reality contradicts what purports to be reason, then it is not reason. Reality is rational, even if people are not.

Our task is not to decide reality, even if we seek to shape reality. It is to observe, discover, and understand reality.

To know and understand reality, we must acknowledge there is reality: an objective reality. There are facts we can generally observe or otherwise sense. Experiences evidence reality.

"*Avoid the precepts of those thinkers whose reasoning is not confirmed by experience*," wrote Italian polymath Leonardo da Vinci, born in 1452, published in *Thoughts on Art and Life* centuries after his death. If experience contradicts a belief, proposition, or idea, then the belief, proposition, or idea is wrong.

With experience comes learning. The experience might be ours. It might be someone else's. To that end, we should consider the possibility that people had the experiences they say they had, even if those experiences do not accord with our precepts: our principles and beliefs.

Hearsay evidence is still evidence, if only hearsay. Its value depends upon the source's credibility.

Experience is more than perception. It is data.

In 1543, Polish astronomer Nicolaus Copernicus published *De revolutionibus orbium coelestium* (*On the Revolutions of the Heavenly Spheres*). Relying upon careful observation of the natural world and other data, scepticism, and inductive reasoning, Copernicus argued that the Earth and other planets revolved around the Sun.

Scientific study applies reason to reality. Science does not need to prove what is demonstrably true by observation because observation is the first step in learning: in science.

In his 1646 book *Pseudodoxia Epidemica*, English polymath Thomas Browne described experiments he had designed and performed. Results from those experiments refuted popular beliefs of his time.

Through the sixteenth and seventeenth centuries, the latter part of the Renaissance, Europe's Scientific Revolution institutionalised the scientific method in the West. The scientific method is to observe or otherwise collect data about reality and ideally draw hypotheses from that data. Those hypotheses should be logically plausible, or at least not preposterous, however improbable or even shocking they seem.

Scientists then construct and carry out experiments testing whether those hypotheses are true, whenever practicable and desirable. Experimental results might confirm or refute those hypotheses. Scientists can then draw conclusions.

Experimental results become more data. Scientists can draw more hypotheses that they and other scientists then test.

Our Scientific Revolution led into our Age of Enlightenment. Born in 1724, German philosopher Immanuel Kant insisted, like da Vinci, that reason not be applied simply in abstract. Reason should be in the context of empiricism: experience, observation, and other data.

The scientific process is endless. The pursuit of truth never ends.

Scientific theory, speculation, and conjecture have value in the pursuit of knowledge, but rational as they are in the light of the data, they are still only theory, speculation, and conjecture. Theorists know their theories might or might not be true.

Examining other people's experimental results, Jewish theoretical physicist Albert Einstein published what we know as his theories of special and general relativity in 1905 and 1915 respectively. Different observers with different frames of reference measure time and distances differently, but it is all objective reality.

Subsequent experimental results supported Einstein's theories. Sometimes, with sophisticated equipment measuring what human beings naturally cannot measure, reality is complicated.

We do not need to be scientists or to use scientific equipment to apply the scientific method. We need only observe and be rational.

Unlike relativity, relativism is fundamentally incompatible with science. Repeating experiments in the same conditions should produce the same results.

Science assumes objective reality. Without facts, there is no science.

The scientific method begins with observations and other data. From facts, the scientific method produces conclusions. The only purpose of science is truth.

Ideologies have come to reverse the scientific method. From conclusions, ideologies produce facts. Purposes are political or social.

Science pursues knowledge and understanding. It does not decree it.

The scientific method does not begin with feelings: people's states of body and mind. Science rejects the presumption that something is true because people say it is true.

Nor does the scientific method begin with ideas, however merited the idea. Instead, data gives rise to ideas, however unpalatable those ideas.

Those ideas might come quickly and easily. They might develop over time, through deep deliberation.

In first instance, knowledge needs no purpose but knowledge itself, without judgement. Knowing the facts, we can consider their implications.

We can decide our response to those facts, as matters of policy. Only with knowledge of reality, perhaps acknowledging that reality is not what we want reality to be, can we seek to forge the future reality we want or avert a future reality we do not want.

Actions can alter reality, but authorities cannot set the rules and assume that reality will follow as authorities wish. Reason judges initiatives, ideas, and policies not by their intentions, popularity, or level of funding and effort, but by their consequences. Those consequences are matters of fact: reality.

There are fields nominally of science in which ideology has superseded the scientific method. Where science fell from favour, observation fell from favour. Facts fell from favour.

Without the scientific method, ideological science deems science to say whatever people want science to say. Believing that something is true, people insist that science says it is true, however factually false it might be. Believing something to be false, people insist that science says it is false, however factually true it might be.

When observation or the rest of the scientific method refutes an ideology, ideological science dismisses the scientific method as pseudo-science: not really science. Ideological science thus dismisses science as pseudo-science.

Ideological scientists are people identifying as scientists. Instead of testing whether ideologies are true, they might construct experiments to affirm those ideologies. They make assumptions and select and interpret evidence to suit: confirmation bias.

If no evidence suits, they can still declare that science proves those ideologies. That has become the nature of ideology.

Other races observe. We need again to see and to listen; to trust our eyes and ears. We need to consider the evidence: all the evidence, including our and other people's experiences.

To restore science is to restore the scientific method to all of the sciences, not merely some of the sciences. It is to reject what the scientific method rejects. If reason, evidence, experience, or experimentation refutes a statement that somebody claims to be science then the statement is not science.

Without reason and the scientific method, our struggle through this Age of Ideology is not simply to gain knowledge. It is to retain knowledge we already have.

"As I reflect on who I am as a white Australian woman and as a psychologist," declared Rachel Phillips, chairwoman of the Psychology Board of Australia, in her *Connections* newsletter of July 2021, *"I also look forward to discovering who I will become as I unlearn the ways of colonisation and learn new ways of walking in partnership with our First Nations Peoples."*

The First Nations Peoples were the Australian Aborigines. Colonisation was Western Civilisation.

No longer do we seek new frontiers of knowledge. Instead, we are retreating from old frontiers. Unlearning and decolonising, we are discarding knowledge we once accumulated.

The Western Civilisation we have become so quick to malign and so keen to dismantle includes reason and the scientific method. It includes Western technologies, arts, and liberties. Driving them to extinction drives the West to extinction.

In place of knowledge is simply walking with other races, submitting to them, not just losing our knowledge but losing our selves. Whatever Phillips imagined she will become, it was presumably not what she was: a white Australian woman; a European woman. It might not be a psychologist, given Australian Aborigines never developed the study we call psychology.

Not only Nazis burn books. From 2019 to 2021, the Conseil scolaire catholique Providence school board in Ontario, Canada burned or otherwise destroyed more than four thousand, seven hundred books to which it objected from thirty schools. The books included fiction, like *Tintin in America*, and non-fiction, including two biographies of French Breton explorer Jacques Cartier and a biography of French explorer Étienne Brûlé.

The school board destroyed literature. It destroyed knowledge.

Not all the books were old. Among them was André Noël's 2000 book *Trafic chez les Hurons*.

The scientific method does not depend on the race of the scientist. It depends upon data and reason.

Ideology depends upon race. The school board destroyed the books for containing cultural appropriation: white people recording and disseminating their observations of other races and cultures.

Whether the observations were factual was immaterial. Being factual might have made them worse.

Prohibiting cultural and other appropriation prohibits us observing and collecting information about other races. It denies the scientific method a chance.

Thus it prohibits the West rationally examining other races and cultures. If those other races are not rationally examining their races and cultures or each other's races and cultures, then nobody is.

Lyne Cossette, the school board's spokeswoman, told the *National Post* newspaper that the books left on school library shelves have "positive and inclusive messages about the diverse communities within our schools." Diverse meant coloured.

The books did not have to be true or even purport to be true. Fiction and purportedly non-fiction alike, the books needed only promote other races.

Presumably anything neutral as well as negative about other races had been destroyed. Perhaps anything neutral or positive about white people had also been destroyed, for lessening the impression that other races made and implying we might not need their inclusion.

Ideology relies upon messages. Science relies upon evidence.

Rational analyses examine all the good and the bad in all races, cultures, and everything else, without fear or favour. Picking only the evidence, if there is any evidence, that suits is bias.

Not only fools comply with the absurdities of ideology. So do people capable of rational thought and discourse, even brilliance.

Instead of exercising their capacity for reason, they meekly follow the mortarboard crowd. They say what they know they should think. It is truth by committee, where every committee member says the same thing.

There was a time we could pay more regard to academic sources than other sources, but our Age of Ideology is nowhere more pervasive than it is regarding academia. Universities are like other human authorities. In essence, they always were.

Science and truth have not changed, but the purveyors of science and truth contradicting prevailing ideologies can no longer readily produce academic articles in their support. Academic roles and grants depend upon academics' concurrence or their silence regarding ideological dictates, whatever they secretly believe.

Academia's role in disseminating ideology is not limited to the subjugation of science. It can taint any field formerly of learning and teaching. Academics incorporate ideologies of diversity, equity, and inclusion into any subjects they can, without regard for the facts. Ideology pervades everything.

There are lines of inquiry that academia no longer undertake. If academics do undertake those inquiries, it is not to learn what is real. It is to try to prove what they already believe, or say they believe.

An individual's intelligence is a matter of fact, however difficult that intelligence might be to assess. Relativism allows people to deem themselves intelligent.

Intelligence is by self-identification: people are intelligent if they consider themselves intelligent. Ideological intellectualism means people appoint themselves intellectuals.

Amidst the power politics that unfold among people conceited in their convictions and contemptuous of independent thought, self-appointed intellectuals deem others intellectual because those others agree with them, or say they agree. They deem people mouthing the prevailing ideologies to be intelligent, at least in that regard.

In that same circle of self-definition, they label people refusing to repeat those prevailing ideologies as fools, at least in that regard. Implicit in that claim is that people need intelligence to believe those ideologies.

Believing irrational ideologies does not require intelligence. It requires a refusal to apply intelligence or a lack of intelligence altogether. It requires deference to authorities sprouting ideologies.

Understanding ideology is reason to question it. Unless academia accepts dissent, majority opinions and even unanimous consensus are meaningless.

Genuine intellectuals might agree or disagree. They do not demand agreement as the price of inclusion.

Instead, genuine intellectuals demand facts and reason, whatever those facts and whatever the outcome of that reason. If we accept people speaking without regard for reality and reason, why would people bother being truthful or rational?

Royal or presidential decree, government legislation, and a thousand peer-reviewed academic articles from a thousand university professors will not make something untrue into something true, or make something true into something untrue. They can only make the truth harder to find.

Reviving our respect for facts and reason would revive our respect for the scientific method. It would begin to revive our respect for Western Civilisation. Conversely, again respecting Western Civilisation, we would again respect reason and the scientific method.

The greater the number of people who read or hear our words and the greater their trust in us, the more important it is that our words are reasoned and true. Our schools and universities especially need again to learn and to teach instead of decide and impose. To be sources of knowledge instead of gatekeepers demanding ideological compliance, our academic journals need again to promulgate knowledge instead of regulating it.

Instead of being process factories for the destruction of Western Civilisation, our universities can lead a revival of Western Civilisation, recolonising the West with reason, critical analysis, and the scientific method. Our universities can again be beacons of knowledge, advancing any race wanting it.

Academics who corrupted their careers by developing and disseminating ideologies can instead analyse the West: how falsities and irrationality arose; how they unfolded; how they can end. Students of those ideologies can examine the fruits of those analyses. They too can analyse. Students and staff can all discuss and debate.

The discussions we have are not the discussions we need. We argue whether pineapple should top pizzas, or whether *Die Hard* is a Christmas film.

The discussions we need, with facts and reason, are about the biological differences between people. They are about the value of marriage and of familial relationships for men, women, and children, along with the impacts of dysfunction and breakdown. They are about adults' and children's vulnerabilities and well-being, in all situations.

They are about human nature, academic freedom, corporate power, and fighting other people's wars. They are about individualism and every other ideology.

They are about anything people want to discuss or debate. My father's cardiologist wanted to publish a letter critical of the Queensland and other governments' over-reaction from March 2020 to the pandemic originating in Wuhan, China in 2019. The Queensland Board of the Medical Board of Australia threatened to de-register him if he did. Time proved him correct.

The discussions we need most, with facts and reason, are about us: the West. They are about everyone else.

We need to consider matters that the Holocaust left us refusing to mention, and increasingly even to venture towards, if venturing towards risked soiling our precious ideologies. Always engaging with reality and forever being rational, we need to discuss ethnicity, race, and religion: ours and every other.

"That multiculturalism is a myth" was a popular debating topic when the woman who later became my wife began teaching senior school in 1988. "There's no way you could argue that today," she remarked, the first Wednesday in March 2024. "The kids are not allowed to say anything other than multiculturalism is a wonderful thing," she elaborated, the last Sunday morning in November 2024. The second Wednesday morning in October 2025, she told me the topic when she was a teacher "generated great discussion. You had the negatives…"

Why did school libraries in south-western Ontario need to ensure that books contained only positive and inclusive messages about the diverse communities within those schools? What did those communities think of each other?

With instead a diversity of messages and children's chances to critique them, or no messages, what would children have thought of those communities? If the children's experiences and their friends' and relatives' experiences defied the decrees of their local school board, then those decrees were wrong, as da Vinci and others from our past understood.

Were Ontarians happier before other races came to their neighbourhoods? Were Canadians more secure before other races came in numbers?

Can Canadian courtesy survive the coming of races not so courteous, let alone rude? Our English good manners are disappearing amidst diversity in Australia. Ignorance and falsehood are not manners.

Can the world-famous Royal Canadian Mounted Police, the Mounties, police every race? All our knowledge and experiences, having regard to our levels of confidence in that knowledge, should be the bases of our beliefs and opinions.

Everything should be up for discussion. If something seems too sensitive, divisive, or important to debate, then debating it is especially important.

5. HISTORY

Judging history is pointless. The value is in knowing and understanding history, as best we can. Learning from history depends on it.

Marie-Antoinette was the beautiful and intelligent Austrian queen to France's King Louis XVI. She donated generously to charitable causes and cared deeply for France's poor, but of people starving without bread, history ascribes to her the words "Let them eat cake." There is no evidence she ever said those words, implying she was oblivious to poor people's suffering, and every reason to believe she did not. History unjustly defames her.

Revolutionaries executed her and her husband in 1793. The West has become Marie-Antoinette.

Learning the facts of the past is generally more difficult than learning the facts of the present; there are more of them, for a start. Understanding the past can be more difficult still.

Like present reality, relativism abrogates any objective past reality. The result of relativism with ideology is a fabricated history.

Ideology is not real. It never was.

For political purposes, ideology has come to denote something historically true that in fact was untrue or something historically untrue that in fact was true. For the West, those political purposes are primarily modern-day diversity, equity, and inclusion, so called.

Ideology is not history. If something was historically true, it is not ideology. It is fact.

Among our past virtues were duty, loyalty, and honour to God and each other: our forebears, compatriots, and descendants. They were duties to defend our families and ethnicities and to develop our cultures and civilisation as best we could, in fact and reputation. With duty and honour came justice and equity.

Our forebears honoured their duties to us. They presumed that we would honour our duties to them, but through the course of the twentieth century, we lost our senses of duty, loyalty, and honour.

No other race tolerates being defamed. We insist upon it.

When other races abandon the truth, it is to promote their reputation and interests. We are the only race demanding falsehoods demeaning us.

For us to insult our forebears for the inheritances our forebears provided us is immoral. It is especially immoral to defame our dead who loved us enough to sacrifice for us: building our respective countries and wealth, fighting for us in war, dying for us.

We owe our forebears the truth, as we owe the truth to ourselves, each other, and our descendants. We owe them and us our best efforts to know what the truth was.

To that end, much like knowledge of the present, our first aim in historical inquiry should be knowledge of historical fact. Having developed that knowledge, we can then decide any implications historical fact might have for the present and future.

Everything to say about reality in the present is also true of reality in the past. Of the past, we need to acknowledge there was an objective reality: people, places, and things existed or did not exist; events happened or did not happen. We can then seek knowledge of people, places, things, and events.

Like the rest of reality, historical knowledge is a matter of evidence. If there is no attainable evidence, then we should acknowledge it. If there is weak evidence, we should cite that weak evidence, acknowledging it is weak. If there is a preponderance of evidence one way or the other, we should say so.

In all events, we should not invent history. We should not say something happened for which there is no evidence it happened.

We should especially not say something happened for which the preponderance of evidence is that it did not happen, as is the case with Marie-Antoinette expecting people without bread to eat cake. Conversely, we should not say something did not happen for which the preponderance of evidence is that it happened.

Historical and other narratives need to be grounded in facts and the evidence thereof. If the facts do not support a narrative, then the narrative is baseless. If the facts contradict a narrative, then the narrative is wrong.

Like other knowledge, public knowledge of history depends upon people telling the truth. Writers and film-makers should craft historical fiction consistent with historical fact. With a background of historical truth, readers and viewers learn truths, ideally while being entertained.

Otherwise, the result is not historical fiction. It is a lie.

Much of the history we have been taught and told is untrue. People repeat that history unaware it is untrue. Our presumptions about people are predicated upon perceptions of a past that never was.

Education and entertainment romanticise other races, while belittling and defaming ours. Our forebears earned our wealth, with intellect and labour, sciences and technologies, and economic and other philosophies. We produced the Renaissance, Scientific Revolution, Enlightenment, and Industrial Revolution.

There was not the racial, sexual, and other diversity through history that education and entertainment presents. That misrepresentation distorts our view of human nature, denying us recognition of the impact of the Jewish Holocaust amid World War II.

Diversity is post Holocaust. Homogeneity is the natural norm.

Around the world and through history, different tribes normally mistrusted each other. Wherever different races encountered each other, getting too close, struggles, tension, and conflict generally ensued, especially through difficult times.

Self-defence is not oppression, as we know when we accord other races their rights of self-defence against us and our forebears. Self-defence is often survival.

All races and ethnicities defended themselves when they could and they felt they needed defence. They also asserted themselves, often by force. Of the various armed invasions of Europe, all but the Turks we eventually repelled.

People of many races enslaved others from their race. They enslaved people of other races. Unlike other empires, the British Empire freed slaves from other races.

Through our Age of Empires, Europe and her colonies brought the rest of the world with us. Providing material, medical, technological, and cultural benefits, we built hospitals and schools, roads and railways for us and other races. We established rights, laws, and civil structures for everyone's benefit. People benefited from rights even if they did not all have the same rights.

There is ample evidence of our forebears' good intentions. *"The British Empire relied heavily on co-operation,"* wrote British historian Jeremy Black in his 2019 book *Imperial Legacies*. We generally treated indigenous people well, seeking to avoid conflict but without surrender when conflict arose.

Our forebears thought they were helping other races. For the most part they did, shouldering our white man's burden.

No other race in history has aided other races more than we have. No other race does so now.

Conversely, there is little or no evidence of cruel motives in our forebears. There is no evidence that our forebears perpetually oppressed other races.

Any other suggestion might be prejudice. It might be a lie intended to manipulate us: a political purpose. It might reflect a desire to understand how races could have fared so differently through history, now that we refuse to think well of ourselves.

We were not perfect, but were trying to progress. The Industrial Revolution improved the lives of rich and poor, but also widened social cracks. In those cracks arose alcoholism that thousands of years of people drinking alcohol and even their drunkenness had not previously produced, along with other problems we worked to redress. Social and economic class divided us, especially in Britain.

By the beginning of 1914, Western Civilisation was nevertheless the greatest civilisation in history: the civilisation of the world. The British Empire, upon which the sun never set, was the greatest empire in history.

We had families, communities, and societies. We had cultures, traditions, and festivities. In the sciences, arts, and learning, we had achieved more than any other race through history had achieved. We were still achieving, presuming that we and with us the rest of humanity would continue improving forever.

We were generally happy. We were generally content.

Unfortunately, we knew it all too well. We took our greatness for granted. We had grown arrogant, cocky, too self-assured to remember that every person and people, however great, can fail.

In 1914, we failed. In the deathly gas and genocidal mud of war, our self-assuredness died.

The Great War accentuated schisms between us. It created schisms within us.

From World War I, two decades later came World War II. Bombs and bullets devastated Europe, the ancestral heart of our colonies.

The world wars bound us through their battles, fires, and deprivations, but their common purpose passed, further fractured us afterwards. Those schisms between us and within us slowly became chasms.

When we see something wrong with us, we might think our faults are innate. They are not. We were the people we are through the millennia we grew and centuries we prospered.

Something changed through the twentieth century. Our view of us changed.

While the flames faded from our cities, the photographic images of concentration camps like Bergen-Belsen in April 1945 did not. Revelations of the Jewish Holocaust shattered our last sense of civilised Europe.

Racial struggles, tensions, and conflict did not begin with the Holocaust. From the Holocaust came blame of our race for those struggles, tensions, and conflicts.

With our white man's burden, we had long sought to overcome racial differences. From the Holocaust came blame of our race for those differences.

Ideology replaced reason and the scientific method regarding race and culture. Influential white people no longer simply sought equality between races. They insisted equality was innately there. It made them feel better.

What began with influential white people came to involve other white people, such was their influence. We ended our mistrust of other races, while they and their ethnicities retained their mistrust of each other. Among races still tribal, tribes mistrusted each other. We trusted all of them.

Discrimination remained. Western authorities continued aiding other races, while slowly losing their last confidences in us.

From the Holocaust came our rejection of racial and religious loyalties, but only ours. The Holocaust made racism and nationalism abhorrent to white people no longer valuing their ethnicity, race, and nation.

Rich and powerful white people separated from each other and further from the poor and powerless white people who Western loyalties had most protected. We ceased safeguarding our families, ethnicities, and race.

Our rejection of racial and religious loyalties became our rejection of race and religion, but only ours. We respected other races' loyalties, presuming that their loyalties defended them from us. Their loyalties only increased with our encouragement.

The struggle between races did not cease because we ceased struggling. As is natural and normal, other races continued asserting their economic, cultural, and political interests where they could.

We became unwilling to assert ourselves. We became unwilling to defend ourselves. We headed straight to defeat.

Weakened by war, we became character-wise weak. We stopped standing for truth and reason.

We presumed that falsehoods and feelings would avert racial and religious conflict. Facts and logic had not.

Our worsening refusal to defend our ethnic and racial interests encouraged other races to become bolder, advancing their interests at our expense. Their pressures upon each of us weakened us still further.

With every passing year or two, we became a little more estranged from our ancestors, descendants, and each other: a little more individualistic. We became a little less moral and a little less kind to each other. We became a little weaker and more vulnerable.

Our disillusionment with our race, cultures, and civilisation grew. We submitted to other races because, ultimately, through the Holocaust we killed Jews.

Increasingly we found faith in money and ideologies. Refusing to engage with some reality, we increasingly put aside more reality. Rejecting reason regarding some matters, we increasingly rejected reason regarding more matters.

Other races assured us of ideologies they did not want for their ethnicities and countries: that they did not believe. Ideology came to consume us.

The Holocaust surreptitiously overwhelmed all other experiences, usurping the rest of history. The years since then have ground us down.

Our malaise gave way to new internecine conflicts. Rather than resist other races and risk racial conflict like the Holocaust, we came increasingly to side with people of other races against people of our race, as no other race does. We became nasty, but only with each other.

No longer do we treat progress as being developments bettering our cultures and civilisation or other cultures and civilisations. We have come to treat progress as being anything that erases our cultures and dismantles our civilisation for the better or worse of other cultures and civilisations, or that erases all cultures and dismantles all civilisations. We denote ourselves progressive accordingly.

Such false progressivism might be Marxism. It might be individualism, if we think we personally gain something by our race's decline. It might be something else.

A century after the Great War, without a chance to recover within ourselves, we have developed indifference and often hostility to our ethnicities and race the like of which the world has never before seen. We of the West were a glorious civilisation. We are not now, but we dismiss our forebears as if ours was the worst civilisation in history.

The facts of history have not changed. Our interest in facts has changed.

Feelings came to matter more than facts. They were feelings that war and holocaust shaped.

We need to understand how so many otherwise good and intelligent white people became so indifferent and even hostile to their race. If they were bad or stupid people, it would be easy to dismiss them. They are not. By this time in history, why are we so willing to let our race decline and die?

Examining history should convince us that we now come from a place not of progress or enlightenment, but of pain and disillusion. Ours is the nihilistic despair that two world wars and the Holocaust brought, directly and indirectly through the decades since then. Allowing and even welcoming our racial fall, imagining something good about it, are our attempts to atone for our past that war ruined and the Holocaust corrupted.

It can never be enough. Thus it becomes our punishment: our sentence of death.

Remaining stuck in a point of history is not progressive. Progress would be seeing our role in Jews' liberation from the camps as much as Jews' captivity. We too need liberation.

Progressing from the Holocaust does not mean denying the Holocaust, any more for the West than for Jews. It means remembering everything else.

It means remembering Beethoven, Byron, and the Beatles, along with the rest of our luminaries. Most of all, it means remembering ordinary Europeans, such as our great-grandparents.

Reversing our decline and fall need not start at the end. It can start at the beginning.

To save ourselves from the mortal wounds of holocaust, we need not imagine travelling back through time to late nineteenth-century Austria to kill a young Adolf Hitler, four decades before he led Germany into Nazism, war, and holocaust. We need instead to imagine travelling back through time to Vienna, Berlin, Moscow, Paris, and London in 1914 to persuade those governments not to start or join the idiot Great War. We need to imagine travelling back through time to Versailles in 1919 to persuade France not to humiliate Germany in the treaty officially ending that dumb war.

The Great War made Hitler as we know him. World War I, not Adolf Hitler, made World War II inevitable.

All else about our decline, fall, and mounting suicide can be traced back to the Great War. In the fallen Russian Empire came revolution in November 1917, the Russian Civil War, the communist Soviet Union, and our Age of Ideology. From France's agony in that war, came the cruelly vengeful Treaty of Versailles in 1919. Together, they brought Nazism to power in Germany in 1933, World War II in Europe from 1939, and the Jewish Holocaust from 1941.

The primary lesson of the Great War is that Europeans should not fight Europeans. Every major adverse social, cultural, and political change around the West since 1914 can be seen as a consequence, at least in part, of the Great War.

That includes most profoundly the Holocaust. Every such detrimental change since World War II is attributable, at least in part, to the Holocaust.

No other conflict similarly scars a race. Our beliefs and attitudes regarding people owe their origins not to reality, reason, or the scientific method, but to the Holocaust. Nothing affects a race more than its attitude to itself.

Generations afterward, most thoughts and feelings unique to the West owe their pained origins to historical moments before most of us were born. War and holocaust shattered us, since which the West has suffered the most caustic, comprehensive, and catastrophic post-traumatic stress in history.

6. CONFLICTS

To understand any conflict, we need to understand both sides' perspectives, as best we can. Understanding people's actions does not mean excusing those actions.

The Middle East comprises the region from Egypt to Turkey and Iran, including the Levant and Arabian Peninsula. Jews are Middle Eastern.

To understand the Jewish Holocaust during World War II, we need to see the perspectives of Jews, Germans, and Nazi collaborators. The Holocaust was far and away the most significant episode since the First Jewish–Roman War in the millennia of mistrust, tensions, and often conflict between Jews and Europeans.

Jews revolted against the Roman Empire in the year 66 *Anno Domini*. Romans destroyed the Second Temple in Jerusalem in the year 70. The war ended in the year 73 or 74 at Masada, where Jewish historian Josephus recorded that Jews facing defeat committed suicide.

Surviving Jews dispersed, quietly colonising disparate neighbourhoods, towns, and villages in other people's countries. Jews call anti-Semitism the oldest hatred. The Jewish diaspora is the oldest diaspora.

William the Conqueror conquered England in 1066. He invited Jews from Rouen to England from 1070 to lend him money and assist him collecting feudal dues, consolidating his rule.

Europeans considered Jews arrogant and greedy. Jews believed they alone were God's chosen people. Both considered the other to be morally inferior.

In 1290, King Edward I issued the Edict of Expulsion, expelling all Jews from England. In 1656, lord protector Oliver Cromwell allowed Jews to return.

Benjamin Disraeli was racially a Jew. He became British prime minister in 1868 and again in 1880.

In 2021, there were those who thought the United Kingdom should apologise to Jews for the Edict of Expulsion more than seven hundred years earlier. There was no consideration of the reasons Edward I issued the edict, or of the two hundred years of increasing anti-Semitism preceding it. There was no recognition that England was English, so that the king had every right to expel foreigners.

There was no gratitude to the English in general or to Cromwell in particular for letting Jews return. The Jews returning might or might not have descended from those expelled. By 2021, there was only the sense that England should always have let other races live there.

Our white man's burden mentality never moulded our relations with Jews as it moulded our relations with black Africans and others. Scattered although they were, Jews did not need our largesse. (Neither did Arabs, Persians, and others less scattered.)

Jews had wealth, much of it ours. In August 2021, professional tour guide Miša Jiroutova, a specialist in Prague Jewish history, addressed a History Discussion Group for Old Knox Grammarians. Traditionally, Christians did not handle money, considering money dirty, said Miša. Christians let Jews handle money because Christians considered Jews already dirty, having killed Christ.

Not only was there mistrust between Europeans and Jews. There was mistrust between groups of Jews.

By the nineteenth century, Czech Jews considered Polish Jews uncultured and uneducated, said Miša. Polish Jews considered Czech Jews arrogant and irreligious.

"*The Jews are our misfortune,*" wrote liberal German historian Heinrich von Treitschke in 1879, amidst growing anti-Semitism in newly unified Germany. While acknowledging Jews' financial abilities, Germans feared that Jews had "*usurped too large a place in our life,*" Jews would never put Germany first, and fundamental differences between Germans and Jews were irreconcilable.

For several years, Bernhard von Bülow, German chancellor from 1900 to 1909, kept a copy of von Treitschke's work on his desk. Von Treitschke saw England as Germany's greatest potential adversary.

The Great War ruined many countries. It ruined no country more than Germany.

German anti-Semitism grew again after Germany's defeat. The weekly newspaper *Der Stürmer* (*The Stormer*) from 1923 until the end of World War II declared *"The Jews are our misfortune"* at the foot of every front page.

"I considered myself German intellectually," said the founder of psychoanalysis Sigmund Freud in an interview in 1926, "until I noticed the growth of anti-Semitic prejudice in Germany and German Austria. Since that time, I consider myself no longer a German. I prefer to call myself a Jew."

After being involved in overseeing the German economy during the Great War, Jewish industrialist Walter Rathenau became German foreign minister in February 1922. He negotiated the Treaty of Rapallo signed in April 1922, establishing friendly relations and providing cover for increasing military co-operation between Germany and communist Russia. Members of the secret Organisation Consul assassinated Rathenau in June 1922.

Communism was bolshevism. In a 1920 newspaper article 'Zionism versus Bolshevism,' subtitled 'A Struggle for the Soul of the Jewish People,' Britain's future prime minister Winston Churchill wrote of national (what we might call nationalist) Jews being good Jews, identifying with the countries in which they lived and practicing their faith.

Churchill considered international (what we might call globalist) Jews, most or all of whom had no Jewish faith, to be bad Jews. They worked *"for the overthrow of civilisation and for the reconstitution of society on the basis of arrested development, of envious malevolence, and impossible equality."* Churchill described communism.

Good Jews' loyalties to their host countries might have been second to their loyalty to fellow Jews, but they fought wars for their host countries. Soldiers being unable to distinguish Jews from Europeans in distant uniform, Jews killed fellow Jews loyal to other host countries against which their host countries were at war.

In Germany, future dictator Adolf Hitler also respected Jewish soldiers. He too despised communism. For Hitler, shattered by the Great War debacle, most Jews were bad.

Among the bad Jews, Churchill named Karl Marx, born in Trier in 1818. Foreshadowing the future, collaborating with and funding Marx was a wealthy German textile factory owner's disillusioned son, Friedrich Engels. In a series of writings in 1845 or 1846, published long after their deaths as *The German Ideology*, Marx and Engels interpreted societies and politics as ideologies.

As much as intellectual analysis, communist ideology was born of feelings, most notably irreligious Jewish hostility to Europeans and our disillusionment. Communism saw history as a struggle between classes, with rich asset-holders exploiting the landless poor. It gave way to a Jewish perspective post Holocaust seeing history as Europeans exploiting other races.

Melding both, we could see history as a struggle between races. Nineteenth-century English biologist Charles Darwin did. He devised the theories of evolution, natural selection, and survival of the fittest.

Nazi Germany also saw history as a struggle between races. Elected to power in 1933, Hitler believed Europe needed defence from Jews.

Colonial Europeans and Jews also suffered tensions. Local theatres around America only showed films complying with their audiences' social and moral standards. The Motion Picture Producers and Distributors of America codified those standards in the Motion Picture Production Code, the Hays Code, in 1930, enforcing it from 1934. Almost ninety years afterwards, a woman of learning at my parish church told me the code arose because Christian America sought to curtail the influence of Jewish Hollywood.

The Holocaust capped a period of particularly fierce conflict between Germans and Jews with Nazis attempting genocide. Mistrust of Jewish anything became unpalatable to the free West.

Fear of Soviet communism continuing its expansion grew. American senator Joseph McCarthy led Congressional efforts in the 1950s to curtail communist influence. Any effect McCarthy had was temporary.

Time alone should have healed the wounds of war. For Jews, the Holocaust kept World War II on foot. World War II became the Holocaust.

Memories spurred Jews to vigour. Memories demoralised us.

The 2018 documentary *The Eyes of Orson Welles* included a question-and-answer session after the screening of American director Welles's 1962 film *The Trial.* Welles was asked the reason Joseph K. behaved so differently and Welles's film ended so differently compared with Prague-born Jewish writer Franz Kafka's 1915 novel.

Welles answered: "…because the book was written before the Holocaust and I couldn't bear the defeat of K. in the book after the

Holocaust. I'm not Jewish but we are all Jewish since the Holocaust, and I couldn't bear for him to submit to death… masochistically… It stank of the old Prague ghetto to me."

The films and television mocking and condemning Western patriotism, nationalism, and racism often came initially from Jews and from Westerners close to Jews, with feeling rather than fact. Jews sought to ensure the West did not commit another holocaust. They punished us for the last holocaust. So did we.

Every post-Holocaust cry for inclusion began as a cry to include Jews. Every scream for diversity began with diversity Jews bring. Even sexual diversity in its origins seemed something more for Jews than for us.

The immediate impact of the Holocaust upon the West proved less damaging than the cultural campaign it precipitated. If we want to curtail the influence of film and television makers, then we should stop watching their product, but they produce it well.

Racial struggles, tensions, and conflict lie behind racism. They also lie behind opposition to racism.

Talk of racism increased in the late 1930s, possibly due to Leon Trotsky's reference to *"racists"* in his three-volume *History of the Russian Revolution* in 1930. Another of Churchill's bad Jews, Trotsky wanted worldwide communist revolution. The Holocaust spread talk of racism.

The Jewish service organisation B'nai B'rith founded the Anti-Defamation League in 1913 to fight American anti-Semitism. In January 2022, the league formalised what had long been informal. Oblivious to the struggles of many white people and the extraordinary benefits that Western countries provided people of other races, it defined racism as *"The marginalization and/or oppression of people of colour based on a socially constructed racial hierarchy that privileges white people."*

Other races remain free to assert their interests in our countries and theirs. They are not so free in each other's countries.

Whatever privilege dominant ethnicities enjoy in countries outside the West, they would not care if races and ethnicities suffering marginalisation or oppression there accused them of racism. Since the Holocaust, we've cared.

There is no universal or enduring hostility to racism. There is universal and enduring racial struggle, tension, and often conflict, continuing unabated.

Ideologically driven definitions of racism deem only white people racist. They empower other ethnicities to advance their interests and cultures at our expense, as if them doing so was virtuous. White people refusing them become racist, even the dwindling numbers of white people in areas that immigrants already dominate and in Western countries already governed by immigrants.

Assailing white racism compels us to be indifferent to our ethnicities and race. Condemning white racism with little or no regard for other racism is condemning white people.

The Anti-Defamation League data base of designated hate speech included any vestiges of our self-respect, such as: "*It's okay to be white.*" Pointing out our lack of self-respect would be racist if it implied we should have self-respect. Is it any wonder that white people ceased believing that it is all right to be white?

Paradoxically, but inevitably given definitions of racism making self-respecting white people racist, maligning white people became anti-racism. Anti-racism became anti-whiteness.

The war against racism is a war against white people, among people refusing to recognise racial struggles, tension, and conflict. It always was.

Historians estimate that six million Jews died during the Holocaust. Their deaths, not ours in war, made the Holocaust cataclysmic for the West.

A similar number of Germans also died in World War II. Their deaths remain largely forgotten.

An ordinary soldier aged twenty from Bamberg, bespectacled Hans Deis went missing in action in Russia in June, 1944. His parents Oskar and Henriette forever mourned their only child, providing for him should he return. He never did.

Lieutenant Michael Kitzelmann was also from Bavaria. "*The only thought and desire of each person is only that the war end,*" he wrote to his parents from Ukraine in September 1941, "*and leave Russia to return to the homeland.*"

Kitzelmann objected to the *Schutzstaffel* death squads' atrocities against Russians and Jews he witnessed from January 1942. He was thus court-martialled for undermining military force and in June 1942, aged twenty-six, executed.

The Nazi regime concealed the Holocaust, telling the German public that Jews were being resettled. Germans compelled to kill

Jews often suffered substance abuse and other mental health problems. Hitler sought to destroy the Jews he feared harming Germany but also the Germans he felt failed him, with World War II obviously lost.

Millions of other Europeans also died; World War II was a civilian war. East Europeans remember their ethnicities' deaths.

Defeating Nazi Germany, Britons and others died saving Jews, although saving Jews was not our motivation. We thought we fought and died to save us: our countries, ethnicities, and race. We thought we were saving civilisation. We were not.

For Jews, the Holocaust was the deadliest encounter in their millennia-long struggle with Europeans. For the West, the period since then is proving deadlier.

Consumed as we became by the Holocaust but forgetting that we were, we came to see ourselves through Jewish eyes. Jews' despair in Bergen-Belsen became our despair. Their hatred of us became our hatred of us.

Without clarity of race among a plethora of races, we melded with Jews. Oxymoronically we came to share a single mythical white privilege and guilt.

Anti-racism and anti-whiteness became anti-Semitism too. People hating the West also hated Jews. Those people included us.

"Never again" was the Jewish cry after the Holocaust. "Never again doesn't mean there won't be problems," rabbi Paul Lewin told a Bring Them Home event at the North Shore Synagogue, Sydney in December 2023. It meant: "The life of a Jew is not going to be given again without consequence."

The deadliest day for Jews since the Holocaust had been the seventh day of October 2023. Six thousand Arabs stormed from Gaza into Israel, happily murdering almost twelve hundred Jews and kidnapping more than two hundred, taking videos and photographs with their telephones. Jews and Europeans have had more conflicts through history than our conflicts with each other.

Rabbi Lewin quoted a man saying that he admired Jews for supporting each other after the attack. "We have had four thousand years of people hating us," answered the rabbi. "We have learnt how to deal with it."

The Queensland University of Technology convened a National Anti-Racism Symposium in January 2025. During a panel discussion on "anti-racist excellence," Monash University doctoral candidate Tasnim Mahmoud Sammak, an Arab, praised the October 2023 massacre of Jews as "an example of anti-racist practice."

If Arabs had massacred twelve hundred Englishmen, women, and children in Brighton, then presumably that too would have been anti-racist. The British government would have arrested English objectors for so-called Islamophobia.

Ideological phobias discredit us defending ourselves and our cultures and civilisation, or civilisation in general. Their roots lie in anti-whiteness,

Having spent more than twenty years tolerating Islamic terror, we expected Israel to do the same. Instead of responding to the massacre of its people as Western countries would of ours, Israel responded as would other countries outside the West. Muslims and Westerners protested against Israel for responding to war with war, for fighting a war waged against it.

People previously prohibited from hating other races and religions found they were free to hate Jews. Anti-Zionism offered anti-Semitism for people refusing to admit it.

The cartoon that Pakistani digital creator Mohammed Subhan Ryk posted on the *Facebook* social media site in July 2024, which my corporate lawyer friend Garry shared, could have come from Nazi Germany, but with Arabs in place of Germans. A blood-dripping animal wearing a Star of David skull cap was eating a baby, while a child wearing the Palestinian Arab flag hid.

The Holocaust consuming Jews, anti-Semitism consumes Jews too, but outside Israel primarily Western anti-Semitism. Western-resident Jews generally neglect the most pervasive and violent anti-Semitism on earth: that from Arabs, Persians, and other Muslims. So do we.

We think of Jewish physicist Albert Einstein, born in Germany in 1879, as the iconic genius. In his travel diaries from October 1922 to March 1923, Einstein commented upon races he encountered.

Levantine merchants boarding Einstein's ship were "*bandit-like.*" Indians and Sinhalese in Colombo "*do little*" and "*need little.*" A "*peculiar herd-like nation,*" Einstein described Chinese, "*often more like automatons than people.*"

"*It would be a pity if these Chinese supplant all other races,*" wrote Einstein. "*For the likes of us the mere thought is unspeakably dreary.*"

Einstein was racist. If we think that Einstein's time produced his racism, then we should recognise that our time produced our rejection of racism. The Conseil scolaire catholique Providence school board would have destroyed Einstein's diaries.

America became Einstein's refuge after the Nazis came to power in Germany in 1933. Nazism made any Western racism a problem for Jews.

"There is separation of coloured people from white people in the United States," complained Einstein in 1946, ironically during a commencement speech at Lincoln University, Pennsylvania, one of the oldest historically black colleges in America. "That separation is not a disease of coloured people. It is a disease of white people. I do not intend to be quiet about it." Jews were not white in America in 1946.

Einstein died in 1955. Faced with the reality of the world seventy years later, might Einstein have spoken of the need for the West to return to racism, but not against Jews?

7. TRIBALISM AND TERRITORIALITY

Tribes can be primitive, developed, or advanced. They can be structured or disorderly.

An orderly tribe is a society. A large enough society or collection of connected societies comprises a nation, ideally inhabiting territory. A large enough nation or collection of connected nations inhabiting territory or territories comprises a civilisation, encompassing perhaps a myriad of nations and societies.

There was none of our newfound accommodation of other races in our countries before World War II. Other than Jews and gypsies seeping in, immigrants to Europe were few. Those that came were curiosities, more likely to be criminals than aristocrats.

Observing the West before the Holocaust and other races still, people are innately tribal. They are also innately territorial. Territoriality is collective because people are connected.

Tribalism and territorialism together make for family homes and tribal lands. They make for nationalism and nation states.

Territories provide food, water, and security. They are places for people to live peacefully according to their cultures, raising their children.

Their territories can be wide-ranging and eternal or small and temporary. Nomadic tribes move around territory they sense being theirs. Gypsies' perceived territory might be parts of Europe for the last thousand years or a park for the coming month or two. A primitive tribe's territory might simply be a watering hole.

In 1894, Hungarian-born Jewish journalist Theodor Herzl witnessed the public humiliation of French-born Jewish army officer Alfred Dreyfus. Herzl recognised that the Enlightenment ideal of Jews assimilating with Europeans had failed. Racial and religious assimilation had failed.

Herzl founded the Zionist Organisation (renamed the World Zionist Organisation in 1960) in Basel, Switzerland in 1897. In 1896, he published a pamphlet *Der Judenstaat* (*The Jewish State*), subtitled *Versuch einer modernen Lösung der Judenfrage* (*Proposal of a modern solution for the Jewish question*).

"*Palestine is our ever-memorable historic home,*" wrote Herzl. Jews were Palestinian.

At the time, the Ottoman Empire ruled Palestine, to which diasporic Jews had already begun returning. They were not colonising. They were coming home: the *Aliyah*.

"*We should there form a portion of a rampart of Europe against Asia,*" continued Herzl, "*an outpost of civilisation as opposed to barbarism.*" Europe was civilisation.

"*We should as a neutral State remain in contact with all Europe, which would have to guarantee our existence.*" Europe would protect the Jewish state.

Jews would protect Christian sites. "*The sanctuaries of Christendom would be safeguarded by assigning to them an extra-territorial status such as is well-known to the law of nations. We should form a guard of honour about these sanctuaries, answering for the fulfilment of this duty with our existence. This guard of honour would be the great symbol of the solution of the Jewish Question after eighteen centuries of Jewish suffering.*"

The Great War ended the Ottoman Empire. In 1920, the League of Nations granted Britain a mandate to rule Palestine.

Winston Churchill's good Jews might well have felt the countries in which they lived were theirs, but in 1920 Churchill already believed that "*by the banks of the Jordan a Jewish State under the protection of the British Crown... would, from every point of view, be beneficial.*"

Waves of Jews returned to Mandatory Palestine, legally and illegally. Britain limited Jewish immigration to appease Arabs.

Amidst their longstanding conflict with Arabs and following conflict with Britain too, Jews declared the modern state of Israel upon the end of the British mandate, in 1948. Jordan and Egypt also took territory formerly under British mandate.

Nation states bring prosperity. They bring survival.

Nowhere are the flames of holocaust fierier within us than they are regarding refugees, but we need to be rational. We need to insist upon truth. No refugees today are fleeing the Holocaust.

Not presuming themselves to be saviours of the world, countries outside the West refuse to admit refugees and other immigrants from ethnicities and religions other than their own or limit their rights, leaving people stateless if need be. Permission to reside and citizenship are privileges.

Countries were traditionally the property of particular ethnicities and races. They still are outside the West, where countries cooperate while maintaining their borders. They exclude people who might disadvantage them, without waiting until people do. They only welcome people who advantage them.

Races other than ours have many reasons to retain their homelands. Those reasons all come down ultimately to their ethnic connectedness and self-respect.

Their connectedness gives them their countries, cultures, and communities. Their self-respect means they want to retain them.

Black Africa is each sub-Saharan tribe and territory and all of them together, although tribal divisions rack Africans between themselves. North Africa comprises the Saharan and Maghreb tribes and lands.

Asia divides into West, Central, East, South, and South East: tribes and ethnicities with their territories. Their relationships vary.

Melanesia, Micronesia, and Polynesia comprise each of their tribes and territory. Often being islands makes their territories clear.

Native Americans, Australian Aborigines, and other indigenous peoples are each of their tribes and lands, united in the face of other races but not between themselves. We used to be the same.

Not only did the sign outside Hornsby Ku-ring-gai Hospital in May 2023 acknowledge *"First Nations Peoples as the traditional owners of these lands and waters,"* referring to Australian Aborigines. It was *"proud"* to do so.

Our pride in Australia used to be in the British Empire colonising these lands and waters to build the country we did. Respecting our roles in creating each of our countries is to revive in us the status we have become so quick to confer upon immigrants.

To treat our race as we treat other races, we would accord our race in Europe the paramountcy that colonial Europeans grant indigenous races. In England, we would proudly declare the English the First Nation People: the traditional owners of English lands and waters. Always was, always will be, English land, we would tirelessly proclaim.

In Australia by August 2025, the Aboriginal flag seemed to be everywhere, often with the Torres Strait Islander flag. In England, local councils removed English flags.

Before Europeans came, the Māori never had a name for the two islands of New Zealand. The North Island they called Aotearoa. Especially through the Jacinda Ardern prime ministership, white New Zealanders took to referring to their country by that Māori name, as if they never were.

Without us insisting our lands are ours, other races claim them. In March 2023, African film-maker Dan Guthrie lived in Stroud, Gloucestershire. *"The English countryside still feels like a white middle-class club,"* complained Guthrie in *The Guardian* newspaper. *"We can – and will – change this."*

The problem, wrote Guthrie, was that most of England remained in private ownership. In time, if we do not recover from the Holocaust, multiracial democracy will elect governments confiscating our homes or our descendants' homes.

Interracial immigration has not enriched us. We were not poor to begin with. We thought we were poor, after two world wars and the Holocaust.

If we think immigrants enrich us, then we should see that European colonisation enriched indigenous races. If we dismiss white people's concern about immigration as xenophobia, then we should similarly dismiss indigenous races protesting European colonialism. If nothing is worth displacing people from their land, then we should see the same of our dispossession.

Other races know their countries are theirs, along with their continents or parts thereof. Again recognising in ourselves what we respect in other races would grant us the same rights to countries and continents that other races enjoy. We would avert our dispossession.

The West is the men, women, and children of each indigenous European ethnicity along with our countries in Europe and beyond, and all of us together. Our problem is our worsening failure since the Great War to feel our togetherness, any step of the way.

Whether the West encompasses ethnic Georgians, Russians, and Armenians and their territories is less important than there being a West. In spite of suffering Soviet communism until 1991, they retained their ethnic connectedness and self-respect: their nationalism.

National tribalism is nationalism. Losing our nationalism, we lost sense of our nations.

Interracial immigration depends upon Western individualism, but our forebears built and died defending our countries not for us individually or for our governments. They did so for their ethnicities.

They did so for our descendants as much as for us. Morality and equity command that we maintain the ethnic homes and heritage our forebears bequeathed to us to bequeath to our descendants, as other races do of theirs. Giving away what we do not own is immoral.

Immigrants can have good intentions. That is no basis for countries outside the West to admit them.

We do not need to see our past as a golden age to recognise the aspects of our lives that have deteriorated with mass interracial immigration. We just need to be rational.

Interracial immigration seems harmless because we deny its adverse effects. Reason means considering the complete impact of immigration upon us.

Morality means considering the complete impact of immigration upon our compatriots and descendants too. Our compatriots would consider the complete impact of immigration upon us. When we could so easily protect our compatriots and descendants, allowing even one of them to suffer to benefit us individually or to benefit people of other races is immoral.

Immigration does not reflect anything we need. It reflects what powerful people want. That might be money or votes, for people who already have plenty. It might be self-congratulation or easing their post-Holocaust guilt. It might be simply another gardener tending to their daffodils.

In June 2024, Jobs and Skills Australia released a draft list of jobs the Australian government believed Australia needed. The list included yoga teachers, martial arts instructors, jewellery designers, and dog trainers.

Australia did not need any of those extravagances. If Australians wanted them, they could pay Australians to provide them. Free markets increase the incomes of people providing services that consumers want, allocating training and the workforce accordingly.

Everything good immigrants do we can do. Countries with obesity problems don't need more chefs and waiters. We have kitchens and supermarkets.

Cutting immigration would alleviate crowding. It would ease

pressure upon public services and infrastructure.

It would aid public safety. Making excuses after crimes occur or police become aware of specific individuals or groups of people planning terror is no substitute for preventing crime and terror reaching so far.

Within the umbrella of individualism lie other ideologies imposed upon Western countries, communities, and clubs, but not upon those of other races. Diversity is anyone but us, however homogenous the immigrant neighbourhoods, schools, and workplaces become. Interracial immigration is ideologically beneficial because we denote diversity beneficial.

All our diversity has done has been to assure other countries of the benefits of their homogeneity. They see the deterioration of Western cities that we refuse to concede.

Immigrants have grounds to celebrate their immigration. If not, they return. They might not have grounds to celebrate each other's immigration.

Having told immigrants that our countries are theirs, they distinguish immigrants of their ethnicity from those of other ethnicities. Other races are not as keen to give away their ethnic properties as we are to give away ours. They exclude us and each other, in their countries and in ours, when it suits them. They are normal.

Our religion and rest of our cultures ought to be our decision. We might not want other races' cultures or elements of their cultures, as other races might not want our cultures or elements of our cultures. To avoid depending on what other races allow us and to avoid risking what they might impose upon us, our chances to choose our religion and rest of our cultures depend upon us retaining our respective countries.

Rationally, we cannot know that we and our descendants will not suffer becoming racial minorities. Willingly becoming minorities in our countries is worse than irrational. It is foolhardy.

Immigrants to much of the West have reached such numbers that they demand we have regard to their race or religion when it suits them. To concur, we should have regard to race and religion always, reporting them in the provision of welfare and services and in respect of fraud, crime, and terror.

We could avert a raft of racial tensions and conflicts if we ceased enticing people of different races to our countries, with expectations they can have what we have. Persisting with immigration when immigrants pound us with their problems is irrational.

Germany accepted ten-year-old Behzad Karim Khani and his family as political refugees from Iran in 1986. In January 2023, after immigrant youths rioted in Germany on New Year's Eve, journalist Khani boasted to German newspaper *Berliner Zeitung* that Germans were dying out. Immigrants would inherit Germany.

No other race would tolerate its replacement. We bask in ours.

Immigrants disproportionately feature in our films and television programmes, our notices and advertisements. They replace our figures factual and fictitious.

We might imagine our cultures and civilisation enduring, but other races' self-respect ensures their cultures will replace ours. At some point, diversity and inclusion always become surrender and submission.

White South Africans are Western, but without a country anymore. South Africa is no longer Western. Whether white Venezuelans and white Bolivians still have countries and whether those countries and others like them are still Western became problematic years ago. They might all portend the end of the West.

Lands once Western becoming lands of other races are not a new West. They are not the West at all. They are other people's bits and blocs, or chaos.

Diversity is our decline. Inclusion is suicidal.

We smile and celebrate the colonisation of Western countries, except when the colonialism was ours. To see only good in other races' colonisation of the West and only bad in our past colonisation outside Europe are both irrational.

If European colonisation was genocide, then mass interracial immigration ushers in our collective suicide: our self-inflicted genocide. We progressed from killing ourselves inadvertently through two world wars to killing ourselves deliberately.

Through it all, weaves the Holocaust. It is understandable for Jews to dwell upon the Holocaust. It is not understandable for the West to do so, while other horrors through history hide among the clouds.

If we want to dwell upon genocide and war, we should remember when we were victims. Africans massacred all the Europeans through the Haitian genocide of 1804. Through the

Armenian genocide from 1915 to 1917, Turks murdered stateless Armenians and Greeks, along with stateless Assyrians. Orchestrating the Holodomor famine from 1932 to 1933, Soviet communists murdered stateless Ukrainians.

The Holocaust is not a reason for the West to welcome immigrants. It is a reason not to welcome immigrants, for that is to repeat the circumstances producing the Holocaust when the world went bad.

The primary lesson of the Holocaust is the inevitability of racial conflict amidst diversity, especially when times are difficult. Had Jews all returned to Palestine before World War II, there would have been no Jewish Holocaust.

There would probably have still been World War II. Britain suffered so much defeating Germany, we also lost. Witnessing that suffering and the West's decline thereafter, perhaps we should not have declared war on Germany in either world war.

The Friday before Remembrance Sunday 2025, host Adil Ray and hostess Kate Garraway interviewed century-old World War II veteran Alec Penstone for the *Good Morning Britain* television programme. "My message is," said Penstone, "I can see in my mind's eye those rows and rows of white stones and all the hundreds of my friends who gave their lives, for what, the country of today? No, I'm sorry, but the sacrifice wasn't worth the result of what it is now."

Recovering our sense of countries being ours requires us to recover our connectedness. We have our ethnic inheritances and heritages, as other races have theirs.

There is no rationally escaping the reality that retaining what remains of our countrysides and neighbourhoods begins with us ending net interracial immigration: admitting no more immigrants from other races, perhaps each other race, than emigrate. Merely slowing immigration merely slows our demise.

Homes for our children are homes for us. Homes for other races are not.

Only we in the West spoil our prized greenery to accommodate other races. If we really cared about our natural environment, immigration would be net zero.

We might not need to block immigration, although other races do. We might need only to cease attracting and retaining immigrants with money and other benefits.

For taking the opportunities our courts and governments give them, we ought not to fault immigrants. They are sensible. We are not.

Talk of human rights creates senses of entitlement. It denies people of other races appreciation for what we give. It denies us motivation to retain what we have.

There are no natural, God-given rights. People have rights because they earn them, individually or collectively, or because other people grant them.

Other races have not granted us or each other the rights that we have increasingly granted all of them. They are rational. We are not.

The only rights are legal. Laws change. Rights change, or disappear altogether.

Rights we have granted, we can revoke. We need again to be like other races.

8. JUSTICE AND EQUITY

Good people can do wrong. Bad people can do right.

Strong and powerful people can do good deeds and bad. So can weak and powerless people.

Strength and power are relative. People weak and powerless in a country can be strong and powerful in their neighbourhoods. People powerful in a country can be powerless in other people's neighbourhoods.

Holding wrongdoers to account for their wrongdoings is just. So is compelling them to compensate their victims.

Punishing the innocent is unjust. Innocent people wrongly labelled wrongdoers are victims.

Compelling innocent people to compensate other people's victims is unjust. Whether innocent people want generously to compensate other people's victims is for them to decide.

Deeming people victims when they are not victims is not justice. Neither is benefiting people in the name of compensation when there is nothing to compensate.

Wrongdoers are not victims by virtue of their wrongdoing. Appeasing wrongdoers might be kind or pragmatic, but it is not justice and probably not equity. Rewarding wrongdoers for their wrongdoing promotes wrongdoing.

Justice and equity need to be grounded in reality, not feelings or perception. Redressing injustice and inequity that are not there can produce injustice and inequity. Alleging hatred and oppression where there is none is hateful and oppressive.

Thus telling the truth and reason are always just and equitable. Lying and irrationality are never just or equitable.

Ideologies denote not simply what is true but what is just or equitable, without regard for the facts. Relativist justice is whatever people denote justice to be, without regard for reality.

Traditionally, we felt fortunate for the innate privilege of being white. With that privilege, came responsibility.

Our senses of superiority over other races inspired our saviour-like white man's burden. We spent centuries striving to save and aid races that our forebears believed on the evidence to be inferior to us, through no fault of theirs or action by us.

Ravaged by the Great War and unjustly humiliated in the Treaty of Versailles, Germany had no mood, capacity, or empire to help lesser races. Needing the assurance of racial superiority to escape Germans' despair as Europeans previously had not, Nazi rhetoric was boastful.

Recoiling at that boastfulness after the Holocaust, we ceased believing in European superiority altogether. Without confidence in our strength and intellect, we ceased aspiring to strength and intellect altogether.

If our presumption of a white man's burden was arrogance, then the arrogance remains. Our past feelings of racial superiority gave way to individual feelings of moral superiority.

Our post-Holocaust white people's burden we call justice and equity. Vast amounts of wealth we dish out to other races: in foreign aid in their countries, in welfare payments in our countries, and in education, health and social services, and charity. No other race feels so obliged.

Equity traditionally meant fairness. It has come to mean equality of outcome, presuming that unequal outcomes are due to unequal opportunities.

We do not expect equality between us and races faring better than we fare, but following the Holocaust, we came to expect equality between us and races faring worse. Attributing races faring worse than we fare upon biology, culture, or anything else differing between races, as we did through our Age of Reason, became known as racism. Racism became wrong.

Insisting we are not innately better than other races, our only remaining explanation for other races' relative shortcomings is white people's racism. Not blaming white people's racism would mean again blaming biology, culture, or something else differing between races. That would be racism. We cannot win.

The Holocaust slowly and often indirectly convinced us to blame everything unpalatable for people of other races on white people's racism. Certain as we are of white people's prejudices, it seems everything we do and have done is racist. The privilege of being white became a fault.

For everyone but Germans, German guilt for the Holocaust

became Western guilt. We treat European ethnicities as perpetrators of the Holocaust and other races as our victims, although collectivising the world into perpetrators or victims of any conflict is irrational.

From the Holocaust came white guilt, perverting our perception of the world through history and the present, corrupting our relations with all other races. The Holocaust effectively deemed us guilty and potentially guilty of any racial conflict, although as a point of law and justice, responsibility for one action does not make people responsible for other actions. Furthermore, guilt is actual, not potential.

Determined not to go to holocaust again, we ignore or excuse other races' prejudices. Whether other races were prejudiced against us, we have told them since the Holocaust they should be. They have every reason to agree.

Recognising reality recognises the races of people making demands of us or wanting to strip us of our heritage and inheritances, along with the contexts in which they do. Our talk of racial justice expresses our irrational white guilt, but from people of other races, it cloaks normal racial struggles.

Behind much we have been told and are still being told lies opportunism. Races understandably want more money, land, and services. Wanting is not justice or equity, but couching their wants in terms of justice and equity appeals to a West that remains wedded to justice and equity. They tell us their circumstances less than ours are not their fault but ours because it suits them.

We believe them. We believe the fault is ours without them telling us.

Refusing to fight, we fail to defend. We have become unwilling to deny other races' accusations against us and reluctant to refuse their demands of us.

We make all the assumptions and reject all the facts we must to assail our race and exonerate other races. We submit in the name of respect, without respecting ourselves or the truth.

Knowing that we do not worry about facts, why would other races worry? If we do not demand that facts support other races' claims against us, then they do not require them.

People pressuring us to help other races even more misrepresent the past and present. When we reward people for lying and concocting, we should not be surprised they lie and concoct.

Other races are less likely to couch their demands of each other in terms of justice and equity, because those other races do not succumb to such demands as we do. In spite of our refusal to admit it, justice and equity are subjective, according to what aids their race.

Justice and equity are subjective for us too, but without our racial loyalties. Post-Holocaust justice and equity are whatever punishes our guilt-ridden race.

Western accommodation of other races is unique. To make room for other races, we push our compatriots aside. We abandon our cultures to make room for theirs. We tailor our laws, governments, and businesses to assist them.

When they complain, we accept their complaints, less they ever feel concerned. When they feel offended, or tell us they feel offended, we apologise. If they tell us they feel aggrieved, that something is unfair, we do all we can to try to make them feel all is fair.

They need not even tell us. We feel their unfairness for them.

Other races do not do the same for us; we do not contemplate they should. They do not do the same for each other.

If we imagine that giving other races more will alleviate their prejudices against us, it does not. It exacerbates them. With us rewarding other races for prejudice against us, why would they not be prejudiced?

When we acknowledge racial tensions, we blame hatred by our race that did not happen in the past and does not happen in the present. Our post-Holocaust frame of mind presumes oppression by white people that is not there. It was never there. Hatred and oppression became political constructs.

We invite other races to accuse us of hating and oppressing them, harming them and denying them their just returns. We punish each other for prejudices against other races never felt, but encourage other races into prejudice against us.

Thus we encourage more racial conflict. Our submission to other races blaming us for their shortcomings drives them to blame us more. We believe them more. We try still more to help them, but still they blame us and still we believe them. We submit still further, compounding our guilt and pain.

None of it is rational from our viewpoint. The lies and untruths, the thinking the worst of white people, is rational for other races because we reward them maligning us.

Trying desperately to atone, we never will. The reconciliation we need is with ourselves.

Without us needing to feel innocent, reason should free us from feeling guilty. We torment ourselves for actions people claim our race has done and does still, but that our race did not do and does not do or that people of all races did and do.

Such injustices suit the people making demands of us. They suit the people who would cripple us.

There is no reason to believe that differences between races are due to white people oppressing other races, especially having regard to the differences between other races. We accredit Japanese, Chinese, and other ethnicities' wealth to their ethnicity, without imagining those ethnicities oppressing races poorer than they are, even if they do.

Ideological dictates of sameness between races ignore the evidence of difference. Some ethnicities are smarter than others. Some ethnicities work harder and more skilfully than others.

Recognising ethnic characteristics would hold ethnicities responsible for themselves. Accountability is empowerment.

Intellect, skill, and diligence are not oppression. Lacking them is not victimhood. Neither are stupidity, ineptitude, and laziness.

Preferring to do something other than work is not victimhood. It might be sensible.

Blaming white people for other races' problems is more than anti-white bigotry. It is white supremacy, for presuming we have or have ever had such power and influence. As much as our white man's burden, it is paternalistic, absolving people of other races from responsibility for their acts and circumstances, while obliging us to help them.

Having created and then increasing other races' expectations that we will accede to them, our sporadic refusals to accommodate their aspirations produce racial tensions, but we need to ease those expectations. To avert racial tension and conflict we need not to fear racial tension and conflict.

People resisting unjust demands are not to blame for provoking tension. People making unjust demands are to blame.

To stop other races making unjust demands of us, we need to cease indulging unjust demands. If we dismissed their complaints against us as they would dismiss complaints against them, their complaining about us would become irrational. Standing up for truth, for us, not for everyone else, we need to find again our racial backbone, which we lost after two world wars and the Holocaust.

Ideological justice begins with judgements, from which people accept, interpret, dismiss, or invent evidence accordingly. Real justice begins with evidence, which people judge rationally according to law.

Much as we require evidence in claims between individuals, we should require evidence in claims between races. Justice founded upon facts requires us to examine, and if necessary argue, the evidence. Accusations are not evidence.

Claimants might not be interested in facts. We need to be.

Meekly submitting to unfounded claims does not serve justice or equity. Not to argue the truth makes us accomplices to injustice.

If we should pay reparations to other races because of our past wrongs, then other races should pay reparations for their past wrongs. We should also invoice them for the benefits we have provided them. They might owe us more money than we owe them.

Centuries of our generosity to other races have not made them generous to us, because there remains no connection between us. Our generosity has not led everyone to like us or led us again to like ourselves.

Our benevolence encourages other races to take advantage of our worsening weakness. Our white people's burden grows and grows.

Instead of seeing the perspectives of other races only in our countries, we should see their perspectives in their countries too. Enjoying their connectedness and self-respect, their ethnicities prevail in their countries.

Why shouldn't our ethnicities enjoy the same primacy in our countries? There is no longer any white privilege, but in Western countries there ought to be, if we are to have in our countries what other races have in theirs.

Instead, other races enjoy privilege in Western countries too. We call it equity or inclusion. It is not.

Diversity, equity, and inclusion as we understand them are for Western countries, not theirs. So is much of the respect for minorities, even submission to minorities, we grant.

Races other than ours applaud diversity, equity, and inclusion, along with multiculturalism, only when and where they benefit. They pursue racial equality to their advantage, not their detriment. They are rational.

Inequality is not necessarily inequity. Equality is not necessarily equity. Collective equity can mask individual inequity.

Other successful ethnicities do not discriminate in favour of people from less successful ethnicities at the expense of people from theirs. They are moral.

Individual differences are unfair. Ethnic differences are unfair. Life and the universe are unfair, without fault by anyone. Trying to overcome racial differences with discrimination against individuals of our race in favour of individuals from other races adds to that unfairness.

Selecting and rewarding individuals on merit is just and equitable. If doing so does not produce equality, then the explanation might be innate.

Denying our compatriots the opportunities their merit warrant is unjust. Granting our compatriots those opportunities is equitable.

Every unwarranted privilege is at the expense of people unprivileged. There are people among all races without skills and education, as there are poor, sick, and other needy.

We feel warm glows of affection to hear of people dedicating their lives to helping refugees and other immigrants or, in colonial European countries, indigenous peoples. Helping people not needing our help especially enchants us.

Equity would be us doing the same for people of our ethnicities. We could spend at least as much time and effort educating, training, and otherwise assisting people of our race as we spend assisting people of other races.

Instead of reaching out our hands to aid the rich and poor of other races because they are of poorer races, we could embrace the poor and vulnerable of our ethnicities and race because they are of our ethnicities and race. We could share our resources and opportunities with the powerless of our ethnicity: helping our malcontent rather than mocking them.

The sentiments would be the same: racism. If we were poor or vulnerable, we would want such loyalty. We might even need it. Aiding the needy of our ethnicity should not appal us.

There is no justice in calling upon a person, family, or ethnicity to give away the wealth the person, family, or ethnicity has fairly earned. Justice entitles us to retain the fruits of our labours and our forebears' labours, much as justice entitles other races to retain the fruits of their labours and their forebears' labours. Equity entitles us to reserve payments of welfare and charitable aid to our disadvantaged, just as other races may do of theirs.

Paying people fair wages or salary for the work they do is equitable. Any taxes that immigrants pay are like board that lodgers pay: fees for living in a country and earning money. Paying taxes need not entitle immigrants to welfare benefits or to free or subsidised services, without reciprocal agreements with their countries.

Expending money to aid other races is an expense on our compatriots and descendants. What other races want, they can pay for, as we pay in their countries.

Nor is there justice in expecting us to give back the land our forebears took without people of other races giving up lands their forebears took. Ideological justice is conquest by political rather than military means.

Ethnicities like to pick their point of greatest reach through history, but all over the world, tribes and ethnicities have pushed their territories outwards and been pushed back. There is no objective moment in time to which we could return every ethnicity on earth, even if we wanted to.

Carrying our white man's burden was never for our poor: people with financial and other practical stresses to consider. Like racial guilt, our white man's burden was an indulgence for our rich: a luxury we could afford when our race was prospering. In our decline, we cannot afford it.

At some point, we need to refuse other races. Like a parent with a child, we need to say no. Denying other races our munificence brings forward what they will lose if the West fails altogether.

Our saviour complex long preceded the Holocaust, but it reached new depths of self-sacrifice through the decades afterwards. Individual self-sacrifice might save an ethnicity, as our soldiers felt in war. Ethnic self-sacrifice saves no one. Racial self-sacrifice is self-destruction, not justice or equity.

Having become comfortable in our unfounded guilt, we need to be bold enough to feel good again. Justice and equity would be us again feeling about our race and ethnicities as people of other races feel of theirs.

9. SELF-RESPECT

We have come to confuse courtesy with respect. Courtesy is politeness. It reflects well upon the courteous.

Being courteous implies nothing about a person's feelings towards people or opinions about them. Courtesy is not respect.

There is no innate right to respect any more than there is an innate right to courtesy or anything else. Rational people only respect people who earn their respect.

Respect can be individual. It can be collective.

Without self-respect, people rarely earn respect, although they might inherit it. We did, for a time.

Mending ourselves requires us to want to mend. It requires us to care.

We need to realise we are worth mending, not just for us and our descendants but for the world. It is the ethnic and racial self-respect that other races enjoy, without them needing to explain or excuse it. Increasingly since the Holocaust, we have needed to excuse it.

Some people recognise themselves as part of their ethnicity and race. Their view of their ethnicity and race contributes to their view of themselves.

Other people perceive themselves apart from their ethnicity and race. That is individualism or sectionalism.

Respect for ourselves does not mean thinking we are perfect. Self-respect is reason to want to improve: to be as good as we can be.

Ethnic and racial self-respect does not mean believing our particular ethnicity and race are better than others. It means not presuming ours are worse.

Wanting our ethnicities and race to survive and prosper does not mean hating or wishing ill upon other ethnicities and races. It means not hating or wishing ill upon ours. Wanting to survive individually and collectively requires at least some small sense of individual and collective self-respect.

That the West has come to be so driven by feelings would be less of a problem if our feelings were of love: love for us; love for our forebears beginning with our parents, or at least with our grandparents or great-grandparents; and love for our descendants beginning with our children. We would love our compatriots, irrespective of whether we agreed with them. We would love our cultures, even if we personally did not participate. We would love our countries and civilisation, in spite of our imperfections. We want so much to be loved, without thinking to love.

Loving our own does not mean hating others. It means loving our own.

The problem with the West being so driven by feelings is that our feelings are of contempt. Two world wars brought us pain, with relief when the dying was over. The Holocaust brought us shame, directly in its immediate aftermath and indirectly through the untruths and part-truths told to us since then.

Our racial self-respect frightens people frightened of our race, comfortable in our demise. We are among them, fearing the war and thence war again and holocaust to which our self-assuredness once led us.

We do not have to like our ethnicity and race. We could start by not hating them.

Indifference would be an improvement. It would acknowledge how little we know.

Racial tribalism is racism. Ethnic tribalism is ethnicism.

Apprehension about outsiders being natural, racial prejudice is natural, protecting tribespeople from harm, but with the Holocaust in mind rather than reason, we refused to be. The Holocaust convinced us that other races could be no worse than we were.

Trying to manage race relations, we became ever more generous to other races and inordinately accommodating of them, whatever ill they did. Refusing to admit their failings, we came in time to deny they could do wrong, romanticising them into ideals of what we wanted them to be.

Other races can do wrong. Everybody can.

No longer asserting the truth, we came to believe people telling us we were worse than other races, whatever good we do. We found consolation through being hostile to our race and cultures, as much of the past as the present.

People prefer merriment to misery. We want to celebrate, but without confidence in ourselves, our celebration is for diversity and inclusion, at our expense. No self-respecting ethnicity or race wants diversity or inclusion at its expense.

To regard our ethnicities as people of other races regard theirs and as we regard theirs, we would declare ourselves proud Englishmen or women and so forth. Our compatriots hearing us would smile.

Pride in their ethnicity remains normal among other races. Pride in ours has become an anathema to us.

As much as other races, we enjoy racial pride. Unlike other races, our pride is no longer in our race.

It is in indigenous races, unless we are indigenous. It is in immigrant races, unless we are immigrants. We laud all the ethnicities and races on earth, apart from the white ones.

We celebrate the achievements of people of other races in our countries, calling them historic, even when they come at our ethnicities and race's loss. We champion the interests not of our ethnicities and race or even of all ethnicities and races, but of other races to our race's detriment.

Other races have every reason to celebrate their advancement. We have every reason to lament our retreat, but the more other races assert themselves and their cultures, the more we celebrate multiculturalism. No other race celebrates its fall, so proud of its decline.

To hear talk of our past greatness we cringe, because Nazi Germany considered Germany great. Fascist Italy considered Italy great, drawing upon Ancient Rome.

That Nazi Germany considered Germans and some other Europeans superior to other races should bother us no more than Imperial Japanese being certain of their racial and cultural superiority bothers modern Japanese. Like Nazi Germany, Japan killed people it believed were inferior and undesirable.

Germany shared our Western rules of war regarding Britons. Japan did not. Through World War II, Japanese tortured and murdered Western and other military and civilian personnel.

Japan did not share its sense of superiority with anyone. It still does not. Western, Chinese, and other victims of Japanese militarism, imperialism, and racism have not affected post-war Japan as Jews affected the post-war West.

Chinese, Indians, and people of other races believing their race to be superior to some or all other races believe that evidence supports them. Their perceived superiority might be biological: physical, psychological, or intellectual. It might be cultural. It might be all of these.

Arabs, Persians, and people of every other race and ethnicity bar us and the Jews can feel superior to other races and ethnicities with impunity, even if they disregard evidence otherwise. They might consider their civilisation to be the greatest civilisation or among the greatest civilisations in history.

We'll echo people of other races' feelings of their supremacy, unconcerned by historical or current reality, oblivious to other races' attitudes to each other. Our submission and self-deprecation encourages them in their conceit. No amount of evidence need diminish their views of themselves.

People do not dismiss them as racial supremacists. They would not care if people did. They might even like it.

No other race rejects any sense of its supremacy, as we now do. So-called white supremacy includes us thinking at all well of our race, remembering the good we do and have done, even if we also think well of other races. It chastises us for not thinking we are worse than other races.

Any sense of our self-respect solicits charges of white supremacy from people refusing to admit their hostility to white people or advancing their race and cultures at our expense. Those people hostile to us include us. Denouncing us for white supremacy has become a weapon wielded against us for defending our ethnicities, race, and cultures in our countries.

We acquiesce, while people of other races assert their ethnicities and cultures in their countries and in ours. So terrified are we of white supremacy, we retreat into white inferiority.

Defending or asserting our ethnicities, race, and cultures, we should no more care about being accused of white supremacy than other races would care about being accused of their racial supremacy for defending or asserting their ethnicities and cultures. We need to shrug off accusations of white supremacy as people of other races would shrug off accusations of their racial supremacy.

Everyone is racist, but to show that we are somehow no longer racist or have somehow become anti-racist since the Holocaust, we have increasingly reversed our racism. We might think that we have risen above all other races, but the problem we have with racism is that we direct our racism against our race: not for ourselves and each other but against ourselves and each other.

Our forebears' racism was from our time of self-respect. Our new racism is from our time without it.

Other races' racism remains unchanged: honouring their ethnicities; supporting their compatriots; benefiting their descendants. Self-respect drives their racism.

Living and working in America, Pakistani actor Kumail Nanjiani used entertainment to promote Pakistanis, Muslims, and immigrants to America generally. In January 2023, he told Britain's *Esquire* magazine that he also wanted to play a villain sometime. "I was told that's going to be hard because people don't want to cast non-white people as bad guys."

Our old racism was casual, matter-of-fact. Our new racism is intense, a matter of identity.

Feelings shaped our old racism and our new racism, but they were different feelings. Love for our race drove our old racism. Contempt for our race drives our new racism.

The thirteenth day of August 2021 on the social media website *Twitter*, American film-maker Michael Moore tweeted: *"From today's news (8/12/2021): "The Census data collected from the 2020 Census was released today — and it revealed that the number of White people in the U.S. has fallen for first time since the first Census was taken in 1790." In other words, best day ever in U.S. history."*

Moore was white. Were white people to assail other races as we assail our race, we would condemn their bigotry. We would call them xenophobic.

We never ceased our prejudices. We simply turned our prejudices against us. We revel in bringing ourselves down.

Reason and the impressions reality made underpinned our old racism. Ideology and the impressions ideology makes underpin our new racism.

To be again like other races, we need to turn around again. Claiming that racial prejudice is never justified while being prejudiced against white people is oxymoronic. Justifying prejudice against white people implicitly acknowledges that any racial prejudice might be justified.

We look back appalled at our forebears' racism, but their racism grew our civilisation for the benefit of the world. Our old racism aided all races.

Our new racism seeks only to harm us, without necessarily aiding other races. Our new racism dismantles and erases Western Civilisation, without considering the consequences. Central to our self-destruction is our self-destructive racism.

Other races enjoy self-love, even if they do not speak in such terms. We suffer self-hatred, even if we do not speak in such terms.

Our racial self-loathing has no basis in fact, but it is inevitable amidst racial struggles when a race ceases to defend itself: to defend the truth. A race hating itself cannot expect relief.

Self-hatred is repulsive. We hate ourselves more.

Self-love is attractive. In pursuit of a people, we cosy up to self-respectful races, applauding them, whatever they think of us doing so. The confidence we once felt in our race and cultures we came to find more and more in other races and their cultures.

During the 2008 American presidential election campaign, Europeans treated black man Barack Obama with messianic adoration. During the 2024 campaign, knowing little about her except her race and gender, Europeans shared a glamorous image of mixed-race black and Indian woman Kamala Harris in the style of New York's Statue of Liberty. In August 2024, French magazine *Runway* called her Lady Liberty. Europeans still revered America, but no longer white America.

Democrats wanted a woman of colour to be the Democratic Party nominee for president. They then insisted Harris lost the election because white people refused to vote for a woman of colour.

They were wrong. Harris did not lose because of her race or gender.

Imagining only good in other races, we disregard whatever ill they do. We love them without wondering why we should. We loathe our race without wondering why we should not.

With us hating us, we invite and incite other races to hate us too. Races can be more hostile to us than our forebears and we have ever been to them, but in our rejection of racism, we rationalise their hostility.

Really, we do not love or particularly respect other races and their cultures. We are too self-absorbed with our self-contempt to consider them.

Self-loathing is self-obsession: narcissism. Self-respect emboldens people to look outwards.

Prejudice against our forebears brought us our self-loathing. Looking upon them fairly can revive our self-respect.

Re-engaging with historical and current reality should spin everything around. Knowing the facts, all the facts, of history and the present would free us from our self-loathing.

Questioning what we are told, seeking the truth, our self-respect is in our hands. Instead of dwelling upon the worst deeds by people of our race and best deeds by people of other races, reason has regard to everything good, bad, and otherwise that people of all races have done and tried to do.

Seeing our race's failings, we need also to see other races' failings towards each other, their own, and us. People of every race have committed wrongs.

We should consider not just the successes of other races but the successes of our race too. We need to talk of our kindness to other races, today and in the past.

Reason is to commend our race at least as eagerly as we commend other races for the good things that people of a race have done. The delight we feel in other races, without mentioning their racial wrongs and failings, we would feel again in ours.

With self-respect, we would celebrate our achievements, such as our arts, sciences, and technologies. Conversely, celebrating our achievements would bring us self-respect.

Reality is often not uniform. Generalisations can be true, as generalisations.

We never ceased being comfortable with generalisations, but sliced from our thinking generalisations negative about other races or positive about ours. What remains are generalisations positive about other races and negative about ours.

Reason is to apply the same collective sense to all, making any generalisation that the preponderance of evidence suggests. Generalisations are still knowledge.

To cease presuming we are inferior to other races, we need to cease pushing aside evidence we are not. Reason considers all the evidence, including evidence that improves our views of us or that we are superior in any way to other races, even just some other races or one other race and in just one small regard. Other races do.

We would find faith in us again. We would find again the joy in our ethnicities, race, and civilisation that we lost in the Great War and lost still more through World War II.

People of other races celebrate their ethnicity, race, and culture. We have at least as many reasons to celebrate ours. Our ethnicities, race, and cultures are worthy of at least the same devotion we give other races and their cultures.

Many causes and ideologies we have adopted since losing faith in ourselves are so plainly nonsensical and self-destructive, intelligent people can only espouse them knowing the damage they do. The only means of reconciling their inconsistences and paradoxes is through the prism of our post-Holocaust despair.

Reviving our self-respect should make those causes fall away. Re-engaging with reason would revive in us the ethnic and racial self-respect to which we are entitled. All in all, we have done very well.

In short, we need to recover from our twentieth-century traumas. We need to move beyond the two world wars and Holocaust: the foundation of our self-loathing, even if we are unaware of it.

We need to see the Holocaust in the context of the whole of human history, instead of seeing the whole of human history in the context of the Holocaust. The Holocaust ended in 1945.

Our decline since World War I, accelerating after World War II, becomes plain. We are not wrongdoers but victims as much of our hubris in 1914 as our emptiness in 1945.

We need psychologically again to be as we were before the Great War. Reality will not lead again to war, because with reason we will recognise where reality led last time.

Self-respect need not produce conceit, so devastating in 1914. Humility and self-respect can walk hand in hand.

Within the mess we now are lies a core of something good, with capacity for something great our ancestors fulfilled, but which the circumstances of our lives deny us. Rediscovering and releasing our good core would revive our self-respect.

Conversely, reviving our self-respect would reawaken our good core. Recovering our self-respect would necessitate us defending and asserting ourselves as other races defend and assert themselves.

Societies and civilisations depend on self-respect. Ethnic and racial self-respect produces individual self-respect, as people recognise their race and ethnicity in them. They produce respect for our species, and what human beings can do.

10. BIOLOGY AND DEFINITION

Above all else, people are important. Thus the most important of facts are facts about people.

Never are our needs to be rational and engage with reality greater than they are regarding people. Nowhere have we become more irrational and disengaged from reality than we have regarding people.

Like bird, fish, and animal reality, human reality is physical. Anatomy and biology are real. They normally, naturally coincide.

We are comfortable with human biology to the extent it is the same in everyone. That should make us comfortable with humanness: human nature.

It is the differences between people we have increasingly refused to consider rationally. The Holocaust brought us fear of categorising people for fear of conflict between categories, but knowledge and understanding of anything depend upon first identifying, defining, and thus categorising. The Holocaust brought us fear of knowledge and understanding about people.

For a time there after the Holocaust, we pretended race was not real. Other races did not so pretend.

Putting aside one observable difference between people, we increasingly put aside more observable differences. Gender ideology is as much about race as it is about gender.

All differences between people became susceptible to erasure. People became susceptible to erasure. Erasing human reality proved the most destructive relativism.

Race remained real to benefit other races or to assail ours. Our Holocaust guilt remained.

We sought refuge from our racial guilt in anything about us except race. Germans had long described their country in the masculine: Fatherland. Fascism venerated motherhood and other womanhood but, like communism, its totalitarianism felt masculine.

German guilt for the Holocaust became the guilt of a Western patriarchy. Western masculinity became toxic.

Masculinity, like femininity, is not toxic. There are good and bad behaviours in people, lots of people, but none of the bad behaviours characterise either men or women. There is no toxic masculinity or toxic femininity.

There is only masculinity and femininity, born of male and female. Much as it is with animals, biological reality isn't simply the facts of male and female. It is men and boys being masculine and women and girls being feminine, as their natures dictate.

Whatever naturally characterises men is masculinity. Whatever naturally characterises women is femininity.

Masculinity and femininity can also draw upon culture. Culture should not defy nature.

Men naturally protect their families and other tribespeople from harm, with force if required. Emasculating Western men suits people determined that we not fight more wars, but it harms Western women well served by Western men protecting them and their families, as Western women once expected of Western men and as women of other races still expect of their men.

When weak-willed men are unwilling to step up on behalf of their families, then strong-willed women do so. When ethnicities need men and women to be warriors, they are.

Imagining men and women being the same denies both of them their differences. To venerate men and women is to venerate their respective strengths and beauties: men's masculinity and women's femininity.

Masculinity and femininity are splendid. Neither is more splendid than the other.

Recognising reality requires recognising differences. Reason in the West has come to require defending basic facts known universally since primitive times about race, gender, and sexuality in the face of ideological absurdity.

Equality is not sameness. People differ. Genders differ.

Races differ. Ethnicities differ.

Differences might be biological. They might be cultural. Culture might be biologically based.

The West did not invent race and gender, as the rest of the world knows. Race and gender came with observable reality: the human experience.

There are no more obvious observations about people than

ethnicity, race, and gender, even if they are hard to discern in some instances. Thus all are immediately scientific.

Whatever the innate differences between races, ethnicities, and genders are matters of fact. Those differences do not depend on the scientific method. Our understanding of them does.

Biology is a science: a rational process of discovery. It is not a feeling or ideology. People are not ideologies.

To dismiss reliance upon biology as biological essentialism or absolutism is to dismiss the paramount importance of reality. A basis in biology is essential because reality is essential. Reality is absolute.

Medicine acts upon reality, developed through biology, anatomy, and other sciences. Mental illness is no less mental illness if it flows from physical abnormalities.

Refusing to believe we are sick does not make us well. However healthy people feel they are, think they are, or identify as being, to dismiss a weak heart or brain tumour as biological essentialism or absolutism is possibly to die.

Relativism might keep us from knowing that other people are dead. It won't keep us from dying.

Beginning with the limbs, organs, and other body parts common to everyone and the biological differences we respect in other species, recognising biological differences between people should be straightforward. Acknowledging there are differences between races, ethnicities, and genders allows consideration of the extent of those differences and their consequences.

Those consequences might be trivial. They might be significant.

In April 2023, my optometrist's receptionist told me she could not wear the Italian spectacles I was buying because she was Chinese. The shape of her Chinese nose would not support them, she said. Thus I noticed the flatness of her Chinese nose and the projection of my British nose.

Nowhere has the importance of defining words become more important than it is regarding racism, because nothing has become more important to the West post Holocaust than racism. Our fixation with racism exceeds even our post-Holocaust fixation with race.

For some people, racism connotes hatred of another race or other races. For most people, it does not.

In 1967, the United Nations Educational, Scientific and Cultural

Organisation adopted its *Statement on Race and Racial Prejudice*. Article 5 declared: "*Racism falsely claims that there is a scientific basis for arranging groups hierarchically in terms of psychological and cultural characteristics that are immutable and innate.*"

Article 5 and statements like it were ideological, purporting to declare truth and falsehood. They shut down scientific and other rational consideration of possible substantive racial dissimilarities, in respect of which we rank people better or worse than others, formally or informally. That included matters of intelligence, criminality, and propensity for violence.

Such statements prohibited people from so much as contemplating biological differences between ethnicities and races that scientists before the Holocaust investigated generally between people. They restricted scientists and everyone else observing people or otherwise collecting data about people. They limited our application of the scientific method. They curtailed knowledge and reason.

Denoting racial supposition and theorising to be wrong mandates ignorance as a virtue. Genes we believe, but we expunge from our thoughts anything important, immutable, and innate potentially related to race and ethnicity. Carefully we create and maintain our ignorance, closing our minds to information.

If we define racism without automatically wanting to prohibit it, racism needs only be recognition of race and ethnicity. Whether something or someone is racist is of itself meaningless. Important is whether racism would be rational or irrational, good or bad, given the evidence and context.

Rational racism aids or protects us, even if all it provides is knowledge. Good racism aids or protects people we are morally bound to aid or protect.

Irrational racism harms or endangers us, even if all it does is deceive. Bad racism harms, defames, or endangers people we are morally bound to aid or protect.

Good, rational racism is natural. Bad, irrational racism is not.

Recognition of reality is always rational, as are inquiry, investigation, and the scientific method. Rationality and irrationality, good and bad, lie in what people do or do not do with their knowledge.

We became hostile to people reporting racist facts or thinking rationally about race and ethnicity, but racist facts are still facts.

Reason is reason however racist the result.

If reality is racist or racism is rational, then rejecting racism is rejecting reality or reason. To be unwaveringly anti-racist is to be anti-reality and anti-reason. That led to us losing interest in facts and reason about people after the Holocaust.

The same can be said of sexism. Sexism needs only be recognition of gender.

How much confusion do we create in children, adolescents, and adults by denying them the clarity of reality and natural normality, especially regarding that most important of matters: themselves? Confusion, delusions, and unnatural behaviours we used to call mental illness, at their extremes amounting to insanity. That included gender dysphoria: men thinking they were women or women thinking they were men.

Sex and gender used to be synonymous. Female used to be synonymous with woman or girl.

New Zealander psychologist John Money separating sex from gender in the 1950s to denote the former as biological and the latter as social did not need to be significant, if gender was simply sociology leaving sex and other biology intact. We did not leave biology intact.

No philosophy of gender or sexuality needed to displace biology, but it did. In our desire to appease the gender dysphoric rather than help them, ideological gender for the West eventually displaced biological gender altogether, at least in humans.

Biology does not depend on feelings, beliefs, or identity. Human biology does not change.

No doctor or midwife randomly assigned my new-born children's genders, plucking them from a list as someone might choose numbers for a lottery. Male or female was self-evident on even the most cursory glance in their direction.

Biology being real, biological abnormality is real. Nominating a hermaphrodite male or female from birth with the dominant gender affirms the basic binary of life.

Absent biological abnormalities, nominating preferred pronouns is irrational. Inventing genders and sexualities is the decadence of an idle rich, even if the rich do not feel rich. Collecting letters into initials and rolling syllables into words do not make them meaningful.

When we shame men for being men or we privilege women,

why would men not want to be women? When we tell women that men are privileged, why would women not want to be men? Men wanting to submit who see women as submissive want to be women. Men or women finding it all too hard might think there is freedom in escaping both genders.

If so-called trans-women can play women's sports and be imprisoned in women's gaols, should not so-called trans-men play men's sports and be imprisoned in men's gaols? Should not the so-called non-binary be excluded from playing any gendered sports and be gaoled in solitary confinement?

All any of it requires is disengagement from reality, along with a profound lack of self-acceptance. It is all very sad, self-abusive, and self-erasing.

Reason recognises reality whatever the context. Recognising race only when it suits other races is irrational. So is recognising gender only when people want to change it.

Engaging with reality frees our time for worthwhile endeavours. Considering the social and cultural roles of race, ethnicity, and gender is rational. Rejecting their biological reality is not. Redefining race, ethnicity, or gender to be solely a social, political, or personal construct, without immutable and innate characteristics, is ideological.

Talk of privilege and power structures is for political science and perhaps sociology. It has no place in biology, and probably no place in anything else except political science and perhaps sociology.

To say that race, ethnicity, and gender are real only because racism and sexism are real ignores the origins of racism and sexism: observable race, ethnicity, and gender. Racism and sexism are among the social and cultural consequences of race, ethnicity, and gender.

Blaming racial, ethnic, or gender differences upon racism or sexism is only rational if there is evidence that racism or sexism caused those differences. More likely is that those differences caused racism or sexism.

Every imaginable effort by the West in pursuit of equality of outcome has failed to overcome racial and gender differences. In seeking explanation for those differences, reason is open to the possibility of immutable and innate differences.

Race, ethnicity, and gender continue irrespective of racism and sexism. Reality continues irrespective of whether people pay attention.

Like racism, sexism can be rational or irrational, good or bad, according to the evidence and context. If racial, ethnic, or gender differences make racism or sexism rational and good but there is no racism or sexism, then there ought to be.

Authenticity lies in reality. People's true selves are their biological selves. Biology is truth.

Meaningful definitions of anything are clear, consistent, and verifiable. They are objective, even if the feelings, perceptions, or opinions they describe are subjective. Of people and animals, they are biological.

Any definition of people not based upon biology is not grounded in reality. It is facile and false.

Redefining gender and nationhood to omit biology is redefining people to omit biology. The mentality that thinks men become women because they say so is the mentality that thinks immigrants and their descendants become British or so forth because our governments say so. They both disregard reality.

There is a politically driven difference between the two. A man becomes a woman if he says he is a woman. The rest of us have to fall into line. Immigrants become British or so forth because we say they do, even if the immigrants do not. Ideological decrees are directed at white people.

Only the West and the agencies we shape define people by their citizenship. Countries become administrative paperwork.

Among races other than ours, race and ethnicity define people. Nations are biological relationships.

Changing citizenship or residence does not change a person's biological relationships. Diasporas are racial.

The only immigrants we don't let replace indigenous people are us. We do not become Asian or African for being born in Asia or Africa. Colonial Europeans remain immigrants, centuries after we arrived; the children of immigrants are immigrants too.

In colonial European countries, indigenous peoples retain their racial, ethnic, and often tribal identities we keep sacrosanct. Realising the same in other races, racial and ethnic identities are all sacrosanct.

Thus immigrants do not become European for being born in Europe. They do not become Western for being born in the West, any more than indigenous people become Western for being born in colonial European countries.

Europeans are the indigenous race or races and ethnicities of Europe. The English are the indigenous ethnicity or race of England.

In 2023, the United Nations Entity for Gender Equality and the Empowerment of Women denoted African man Munroe Bergdorf its first United Kingdom Champion woman. To redefine women to include men or to redefine British to include Africans is like redefining trees to include sponge cakes.

Also in 2023, the Scottish National Party elected Humza Yousaf its leader, making him the First Minister of Scotland. The United Kingdom, Ireland, and other Western countries had elected immigrants their leaders, but Yousaf stood at the helm of a supposedly nationalist political party.

In January 2024, Yousaf faced Nick Robinson of the British Broadcasting Corporation programme *Political Thinking*. Yousaf said that he had never been comfortable with the Scottish National Party's name because it could be "misinterpreted." He said "we are a civic national party." It did not "matter where you come from."

Imagining that citizenship or residency connects people is civic nationalism, but plainly citizenship and residency do not connect people. Citizenship and residency do not connect us anymore, let alone connect people of different races.

Civic nationalism is another wishful Western fantasy, this one predicated upon our rejection of biological relationship but also our tacit recognition of the benefits of nationalism. This fantasy delivered Yousaf the leadership of Scotland.

Denying our countries our ethnic definitions denies us our countries. It erases our ethnicities. Way worse than a mere lack of self-respect, mass interracial immigration and redefining our countries without us are the means of our mass racial replacement, without us ever being meant to notice.

We do notice, but only to like it. Lacking our self-respect, we presume that other races make our countries modern.

They do not. They make our countries other people's countries, or nobody's countries.

Modern can mean us, if we want it to. Modern Japan, China, and so forth are all still Japan, China, and so forth, without distraction from other races and ethnicities.

We need to recognise more than concepts of race, ethnicity, and gender. We need to recognise specific races, ethnicities, and genders.

Other races recognise themselves. They survive. Some prosper.

We recognise them too. We care for them. We want them to prosper.

Caring about a race or ethnicity, wanting it to prosper, is racist. That race or ethnicity could be ours, if we let it.

We are not surviving. Without recognising our race and ethnicities, there is still genocide, but lost in a great global populace, we are unaware we are dying.

Other races know race, ethnicity, and gender are real. Inside, we know too. We have become selective about when we acknowledge them.

We need to lose our last pretence. It is not a matter of sounding all very reasonable but being racist or sexist. It is a matter of being racist or sexist whenever being so is rational.

11. CONNECTION AND IDENTITY

Animals co-operate with their kind. They pack and herd. Fish swim in schools. Birds fly in flocks. Insects live in nests, hives, and other colonies.

Alone in their natural habitats, animals are vulnerable to being killed. Without their packs, predators become prey. In their herds, prey can be predatory.

It is the same with people. The herd instinct in animals is the tribal instinct in humans, feeling part of a people more than a person's individual self, safeguarding tribespeople from internal and external threats.

The human species comprises races. Races can comprise ethnicities. Both comprise families.

Family, ethnicity, and race are biological connections between people, making them natural tribes. Concentric biological tribes are compatible because they are concentric. Belonging to one is normally belonging to the next.

Following the French Revolution in 1789, Irish-born British statesman Edmund Burke wrote *Reflections on the Revolution in France*. He described society as *"a partnership not only between those who are living, but between those who are living, those who are dead, and those who are to be born."*

The classic individualism of colonial Europeans was useful self-reliance in alien and often hostile environments. Individualism became a problem when we lost our tribalism: our partnerships.

Victories and defeats are collective when people feel connected. They know that what happens to their family, ethnicity, and race happens to them. Tribalism separates people from people of other tribes, but connects them with their tribespeople.

Individualism, as it has come to be, makes everything personal. Individualism separates each of us from everyone.

No other race thinks or feels as we do. Before the two world wars and Holocaust, neither did we.

Traditionally, collectivist cultures were ethnically and religiously homogenous. To talk of primitive societies being communist needs to recognise their ethnic and religious homogeneity, as remains normal outside the West.

Following the Great War, Soviet communism imposed upon the former Russian Empire the idea that people across different races and religions could form a multi-racial, irreligious collective. The ultimate vision was globalism: a single-world civilisation, without racial, religious, or national borders.

In spite of propaganda otherwise, Soviet communism failed. We might imagine connecting with a shared humanity amidst racial and religious diversity, but self-respecting people do not maintain their generosities when humanity does not reciprocate. The only sustainable collectivism has proven to require tribalism.

Connectedness need not mean collectivism. It did not through our Age of Enlightenment; we were individuals in partnership. Connectedness can simply be consciousness of being a family, ethnicity, and race.

Only in contrast with disconnectedness does connectedness mean anything. Connectedness is tribalism.

Disconnectedness is individualism: brokenness. Hyper-individualism is still individualism.

Repairing what broke in the Great War means reconnecting what parted after World War II: us. The Holocaust, not science, led the West to separate each of us from the rest of our ethnicity and race, disregarding our biological relationships.

Relativism erased biological relationships altogether. Parenthood, family, and people became whatever anybody wanted them to be. Without objective definition, they became meaningless.

Our separation widened and deepened over time. Uninterested in their compatriots, who in turn were uninterested in them, our young grew up without experiencing connection and belonging.

Western connectedness ended, as our separatism slowly became complete, with all that separatism entails. We have become the most divided race on earth, the most isolated people in history, ultimately turning us against our forebears, each other, and our descendants.

For parenthood and other familial relationships to be meaningful, they need to be real. To be real, they need to be biological.

Anything else is a metaphor. Metaphors are not reality.

Talk of community does not create community. Community, society, and civilisation depend upon connectedness.

Commonality alone is not connection. We have to feel connected with our fellow tribespeople if we want our fellow tribespeople to keep feeling connected with us. Connectedness is mutual.

Poorly satisfied by the flimsy tribes of football fandom and the like, our tribal instincts remain. We are no less innately tribal than people of other races, but we have succumbed to tribal-like divisions pitting portions of our families, ethnicities, and race against our own.

We might imagine those unnatural divisions connecting us with people of other races. They do not.

People of other races remain connected with their family, ethnicity, and race. We used to complain about them sticking together in their communities, before we stopped complaining about other races.

We took to complaining about our race. Post Holocaust, white people only complain about other white people.

Other races congregate not because of white people's prejudice but because tribespeople naturally congregate. We used to do so too.

Races and often ethnicities are big. That makes them strong.

Tribespeople enjoy the power of their people. In the struggles and competitions of the world, races and ethnicities prevail over individuals by their co-operation and weight of numbers, whoever the races and ethnicities and whoever the individuals. When need be, tribespeople stand, work, and struggle together against outsiders. Tribalism is unity.

Individuals are small. That makes us weak and anxious.

Without tribes supporting us, we measly individuals became physically, mentally, and emotionally vulnerable to people of other races and to rogues among our race. It is the root of our loneliness, fragility, and fall.

All our individualism has done is to assure other races of their tribalism. All our rejection of our race has done is to embolden other races.

Ego is not strength. Connection is. Connectedness brings people emotional and material relief from the smallness of individualism.

Individualism is narcissism. The cure for narcissism is not globalism, because globalism always reduces to individualism. The cure for narcissism is tribalism, drawing people into something bigger than their individual selves.

Collective self-determination depends upon there being a collective self. Communities are racially and religiously homogenous or close to it.

There are no multicultural communities. Different races do not gel into single societies.

The best that can happen is that a community allows people from other ethnicities and races to mingle: visiting, living, or working. Societies might absorb small numbers of those people, especially from related ethnicities. They might not.

However much we try to connect and remain connected with people of other races, and however much we might presume we are connected, racial and religious pluralities devolve in practice to racial and religious sectarianism or individualism. There is no connectedness in diversity.

Not only is there no connection between races, racial diversity disconnects people within races, no race more than ours. Communities break down. Countries break down.

Having lost our connectedness with the rest of our ethnicity and race, we do not notice our disconnectedness with people of other races, but we never had to work so hard to foster social cohesion when we had social cohesion. We try to hold people together with money, but in time, the money runs out.

At best, people co-operate in the contexts of common interests. Few interests remain common for long.

Ideologies of inclusion are not connectedness. They place people beside each other, unable to connect them.

Proximity is not togetherness. Trumpeting our inclusion of people feeling no connection with us is a fraud we perpetrate against us.

Inclusion depends upon a common tribalism. Conversely, tribalism produces inclusion: inclusion of fellow tribespeople. The inclusion we need is of us.

Tribalism excludes people outside the tribe. Individualism excludes everyone.

Communism contemplated conflict-ridden tribalism by class, wealth, and job. It failed. Poverty does not connect people for long.

However much we hope or are certain otherwise, tribalism and individualism are people's only practical choices. If we are not to remain alone in the world, the connections we respect in other races we need to respect again in ours. We need to reconnect with people with whom we are related.

Families are the closest of connections. Our first connection in life with other people is with our parents: the starting point of connectedness.

However deeply we might feel intertwined with our spouse, the means by which spouses become closely connected is by bearing children together. People with whom each spouse is closely connected then also become closely connected.

The most substantive and enduring connectedness has proven to be biological. Relatives are biological connections, unaltered by whether we meet.

Biological relationships become biological tribalism, if we let our kin connect us as kin of other races connect them. They relish their nepotism.

Reaching through generations, biological relationships connect people with their forebears and descendants. To treasure our parents, grandparents, and so forth is to treasure their other children, grandchildren and so forth.

Immediate families spread outwards into clans, although few families have recourse to clans. Expanding arrays of cousins ease as far as homogeneity allows into ethnicities.

Families are too small to survive in isolation. Families need ethnicities too.

Any purported community not based upon biology is brittle, superficial, and transient. For comfort, security, and strength, each of us needs a family, ethnicity, and race. The rest of our family, ethnicity, and race need us.

Ethnic connectedness is ethnicism. Racial connectedness is racism. Family, ethnicism, and racism are biological tribalism.

Rejecting racism is individualism, with its isolation, immorality, and vulnerability. Identifying with our respective family, ethnicity, and race is rejecting individualism.

Ethnicism and racism connect people otherwise divided by class, wealth, or vocation, or by age, gender, or politics. The factors by which people congregate socially need not divide them.

Within each ethnicity and race, ethnicism and racism facilitate equality of opportunity and equity. They encourage tolerance, discouraging discrimination and prejudice.

Biological connectedness does not depend upon people's manners or beliefs. Multiculturalism among a race and ethnicity encompasses young and old people's cultures, rich and poor people's cultures, and city, rural, and regional cultures.

Allowing diversity of thought, freeing us to think independently, racism and ethnicism connect people who disagree. We remain connected, however stupid or awful we think our fellow tribespeople are and however awful or stupid they think we are.

In many contexts, we already dispense with our individualism and resume our racial connectedness. Our problem is that those contexts are all bad.

We respect race when it requires us to help other races or neglect our own. We are tribal when it comes to feeling shame for what we think our ethnicity or race has done or does.

The only racism that troubles races other than ours is racism explicitly or implicitly against their race or ethnicity. That is rational.

People of any race worrying about racism that favours or defends their race or ethnicity are being irrational. Only we do. Only we hate our own for admiring or aiding our ethnicity, for liking or loving our race.

Ultimately, we do so because Nazis killed Jews. Blaming World War II upon Germany instead of blaming us all in the Great War, paradoxically we fear Nazis and yet we feel guilty for the Holocaust.

Our fear has been irrational at least since 1945. Our guilt fails to have regard for the rest of history.

Respecting a race respects its racism furthering that race. Fighting a race fights its racism safeguarding that race.

There is nothing we now find more virtuous than our complete opposition to racism: our vehement opposition to our race. Yet, there is no surer affirmation of our countries, cultures, and races than through our hostility towards them.

The perpetual struggle, tension, and conflict between races, often with us under the pretence of fighting white people's racism, ought to persuade us that race is and will remain the primary human identity, however determined we often are to ignore it. We can like, love, or loathe race, including our own, but we cannot ignore it.

Race is inescapable. People of other races might not mention race when mentioning race does not suit them, but their silence does not make race any less their identity. They do not need us to notice for them to notice.

Like so much else about other races, we respect their racial identities, whenever it suits them. Only our racial identities make us uncomfortable, as they have increasingly done since the Holocaust. Our post-Holocaust grasp for identity is a grasp for a post-racial identity.

Nowhere is our need to re-engage with reality more in evidence than it is regarding identity. Identities grounded in reality do not require validation, whatever that means, or affirmation.

Identity should be simple. It should be immutable.

Identifying with all humanity is not identity. It is a lack of identity.

To insist that human beings are either individuals or a single human species with nothing in between leaves us as individuals. It leaves us alone.

Identity lies in connection. There is no identity in diversity.

Tribalism provides a common identity in being part of the tribe. From our natural, concentric tribes come our natural, concentric identities.

With our families, ethnicities, and race again defining us, dictating our identities, we can relinquish those post-racial identities that for us replaced race. Those post-racial identities gave us nothing in return, leaving us alone.

Gender need not be an identity. It can simply be a fact.

Race and ethnicity can also be simply facts, but with ethnic and racial identities, at least those we want, there is no need for gender identities, destructive as they are. Biological relationships connecting us mean that biological differences need not divide us.

Racial identities save people from seeking identity through silly games, especially word games, inventing genders and sexualities. The cry for identity is the cry for attention among people feeling they need attention or identity.

Blonde-haired German model Martina Big was born in 1988. In December 2012, she underwent the first of twenty-three procedures inserting implants increasing the size of her breasts. In

January 2017, she underwent surgery to look like a black woman. In February 2018, she travelled to the town of Nyeri in Kenya, where pastor Isaac Murage of the Gichira Baptist Church baptised her with the Swahili name Malaika Kubwa, declaring her to be a true African woman.

Big did not deny race. She affirmed race, albeit superficially.

So did Englishman Oli London, born in 1990. He supported the black nationalist Black Lives Matter movement.

From 2013, London lived in South Korea for about a year teaching English. Afterwards, he spent a hundred thousand dollars on cosmetic surgery to appear Korean. That surgery included lip fillers, blepharoplasty, genioplasty, and rhinoplasty; race is much more than skin colour. In 2021, London declared he was transracial.

London also declared himself non-binary. In mid-2022, he declared he was a gender-fluid transwoman.

Big and London embraced race, but not their own. Their race they rejected. London also rejected his gender.

London recovered. In October 2022, he announced he was a man again. He ceased undergoing surgery.

He wrote the 2023 book *Gender Madness*. In July 2024, London wrote on *Instagram* social media that Black Lives Matter, gender ideology, and the Free Palestine movement had "*one thing in common – Marxism.*"

They all amounted to anti-whiteness, although Marx did not doubt racial differences or dismiss their significance, as Marxists post Holocaust have increasingly done. If the Marxists of 2025 knew what Marx said of race, they would cancel Marx too.

An observable correlation had developed among white people advocating for other races and engaging in ever more aberrant behaviour. People thinking that progress requires them to reject their forebears and everything their forebears believed, as we have done increasingly with each generation since the Great War and especially since the Holocaust, have become more and more irrational.

People rejecting their forebears reject themselves. People neglecting their descendants neglect themselves.

They become ever more self-destructive. In their essence, successive ideologies have sought increasingly to tear down Western Civilisation, whether in the West or in Israel.

Our mocking and damning our preceding generations teaches our subsequent generations to mock and damn us. People who allow their forebears no excuse should expect their descendants to allow them no excuse.

As the rest of the world knows, deriding our forebears or neglecting our descendants is not progress. It is individualism.

We need to unfurl again the biological connectedness that every other race but ours never surrendered or suppressed. As people of other races honour their ancestors, reconnecting with our ancestors should lead us to honour ours.

Seeking truth, we might disagree with our ancestors. Agreeing with them, we would defend their reputations

At this stage in our histories, we might do well to disagree with our parents. Rejecting our parents' beliefs is tantamount to embracing our parents, when our parents' beliefs amount to them rejecting themselves.

We cannot value our people if we have no sense we are a people. We cannot value our family, ethnicity, and race without recognising we have a family, ethnicity, and race. We cannot value the West without recognising there is a West.

Valuing each, we value ourselves. We mend.

With human beings' innate tribalism leading people to form mobs of some form or another, we cannot keep our ideological mobs from being mobs. With ethnicity and race re-uniting us, we can keep our mobs from being ideological, fighting us.

12. LOYALTY AND COMPATRIOTISM

Other races but ours enjoy nationalism, patriotism, and compatriotism. They are all natural connectedness. They are all natural tribalism.

Nationalism is intellectual. It is recognition of the benefits to people of the same race or ethnicity coming together to form a country. It is people's identity in and support for their country, race, or ethnicity.

Patriotism is emotional. It is people's love for their country.

Compatriotism is personal. It is each person's loyalty towards each other person of his or her country, race, or ethnicity.

Compatriots are tribespeople. Compatriotism is rational and mutually beneficial.

Loyalty does not mean protecting rogues. Our loyalty to the rest of our compatriots might mean punishing or isolating rogues.

Tribalism inspires loyalty. National loyalty is nationalism. Ethnic loyalty is ethnicism. Racial loyalty is racism.

People of other races but ours generally co-operate with their own, possibly helping their own but at least not wilfully neglecting their own to help outsiders. We used to be the same.

We respect people of other races discriminating in favour of others of their ethnicity or race – patronising their businesses, employing their own – however much it means us missing out. We might discriminate in their favour too.

Racial loyalty we still espouse, but our loyalty is no longer to our race. It is to indigenous races, unless we are the indigenous race. It is to immigrant races, unless we are the immigrant race.

Whether loyalty to other races is rational depends on the race, but a higher loyalty to another ethnicity or race than our own is never rational. Disloyalty to our relatives and compatriots loyal to us is irrational, unjust, and inequitable. Whether that disloyalty is for ideology, momentary profit, or feelings of self-righteousness is immaterial.

Loyalty is not fealty. If we want loyalty, we have to give loyalty.

Were we still like other races, instead of delighting most in the success of people of other races, we would delight most in the success of people of our ethnicity and race. We too might discriminate in favour of our own. (Laws need to let us do so.)

Discrimination need not take anything away from other races. It might be us not giving them so much.

Human authorities' success in corrupting us into the people they want us to be took advantage of our societies' breakdown after war. Authorities convinced us that our nationalism – our connectedness – took us to war, but our connectedness did not take us to war. To the world wars in Europe, our governments took us.

Nationalists might blunder into war; everyone can err. Nationalists do not remain unnecessarily in war, killing their compatriots.

To World War II in Asia, Japan took us. Japanese nationalism continues to serve Japan well. Its militarism starting World War II in Asia did not.

Our connectedness with our compatriots defended us from wars that other people waged against us. Yet, we have come to mistrust our compatriots while trusting those other people, provided those other people are from another race.

Instead of treating white racists as pariahs, we could wonder why we do. We could wonder what brought us to this point.

Throughout our Age of Ideology, ideologies have spread not through debate and persuasion, but through propaganda. The winds of ideology have blown increasingly hard against us.

There is an extraordinary conformity of expression in a West where nothing has come to matter more than ideology. Advocates know only to say read a book or watch a television programme, as if being in a book or on a television screen makes something untrue into something true. Lies become treated as truths because those lies came in a book. Falsehoods become treated as facts because they appeared on a screen.

Critical analysis requires stepping back from the endless euphoria pumped up for irrationalities. Reason requires examining the differences called diversity before accepting those differences. Even the most rudimentary of questioning realises that blithely insisting there are no differences between races, genders, and cultures or that insisting those differences are immaterial makes celebrating those differences illogical.

Irrational ideologies depend upon de facto dictatorship, denying people facts and reason. Sometimes subtly exerting their cruellest control, despots determine what people believe.

Totalitarianism can seem soft. Tyrants can seem sweet.

It is a great shame that British writer George Orwell titled his 1949 novel *Nineteen Eighty-Four*. Most people since the year 1984 have failed to see increasing around them the phenomena Orwell described: powerful people's manipulation of language; the uniform, incessant, and all-pervasive political messaging; the lies as truth and truth as lies; the populace's soulless submission.

Early in the twenty-first century, Orwell's novel could be republished every year with the title of a year soon coming. Darkness is enlightenment but our Enlightenment was darkness. Strength is weakness and weakness is strength. Shame is pride but pride is shame. Love is hate and hate is love.

Decline is progress. Delusion is reality. Fantasies are facts.

Authorities saturate us with cries not for us but for diversity and inclusion, at our expense, and at the expense of nature, normality, and morality. They flood us with unimportant truths and the most damaging of untruths, especially related to race, religion, gender, and sexuality. They deluge us with enthusiasm for other races and cultures but contempt for our race and cultures, defaming and diminishing us.

To submit to ideologies is to enjoy the public adoration of others who submit. Authorities sanctify compliance and people who comply.

Thus people seeking to reduce and erase our race, cultures, and countries can expect others to laud them for their progressivism. They can expect applause from races doing well from our celebratory death wish, however much those races might hold us in bewilderment. Other races in our presence repeat those dictates too, but don't believe or teach their children anything that harms them.

Whether our compatriots believe what they say, only they know. When we say something so often that we start thinking it, we might not know what we believe. An Orwellian dystopia was more obvious to observe in other countries before it became real around us.

Without biological connectedness, we have become less and less concerned with whether the rest of our race lives or dies. We have become more and more consumed with what the rest of our race says, thinks, and feels.

Our rights to free speech are ideological rights: to tell people of our race what to say. We have the right to enforce every prevailing ideology against family, friends, and strangers alike, whatever we secretly believe.

Authorities uninterested in protecting Western ethnicities and cultures have become preoccupied with policing Western people's feelings and beliefs. The rule of ideology denotes not just what is true, but what is proper.

Controversial has become an insult for dissent, or simply for views, feelings, and ideas failing to celebrate prevailing ideologies. Facts, reasoning, and morality refuting those ideologies have become offensive.

Irrational ideologies cannot withstand battles of ideas with facts and reason. Authorities thus stifle the battles altogether. With shaming and law, they demonise dissent and dissenters.

Our talk of diversity and inclusion are lies. There is no diversity of feelings, thoughts, or viewpoints, when it comes to anything important. There is no inclusion of our own, when our own fall afoul of a prevailing ideology. Demands for diversity disappear amidst our displeasure or discontent.

We do not fight other races; that would be racist. We fight our race, as we did in Europe through World War II. Becoming increasingly reluctant to struggle with other races after the Holocaust, we became increasingly confined to conflicting with our race.

In August 2021, *British Broadcasting Corporation News* published a story titled 'The giant puppet walking 5,000 miles to the U.K.' No story is too stupid to publish when its emotional impact is to promote Western acceptance of immigration. *"Meet Little Amal,"* the *Facebook* social media website introduced the story, *"the not so little puppet of a 9-year-old Syrian girl who is following the journey made by millions of child refugees who have fled the war in Syria."*

Those children were not headed to fellow Arab countries nearby. They were headed to Europe.

In a similarly stupid vein, I commented: *"How about the giant puppet stay home with her people."* Twenty-nine people liked my comment. Four people loved it. Ten people were angry. Four people laughed. Whatever people thought of human immigration, they could laugh at a comment about puppet immigration.

Not only must we welcome human immigrants, we must welcome puppet immigrants too. My comment set forth the usual abuse upon anyone Western not welcoming immigrants, calling me ugly and with evil in my eyes. Had I welcomed the puppet, those same people would have seen my face and eyes differently. "*Your interior for sure matches your exterior,*" wrote Kevin Newin.

"*I like how you make fun of his physical appearance,*" Nathan Hanscom replied to Kevin, "*while trying to show yourself as being morally superior, but don't see the irony.*"

"*ok boomer,*" Kevin replied to Nathan.

Boomer was the usual pejorative dismissing white people of the baby-boomer generation, generally defined as those born from 1946 to 1964, immediately after World War II. People appalled at racism were freely prejudiced against older white people, many of whom dismayed at the decline of their countries they had witnessed since their youth.

Yet none of the comments were as interesting as the response of one woman who did not comment on *Facebook*. Nor did she express any liking, loving, anger, or laughing at my comment.

Instead, Imogen MacQuarrie seems to have checked my profile page on *Facebook*, or perhaps on the *Linked In* social media site to which my *Facebook* profile included a link. She saw that I consulted to a professional association. She thus contacted Rona, the association's president, through the association website.

"*Do you realise your 'consultant' Simon Lennon is putting racist comments on social media?*" Imogen wrote to Rona. "*Have a look at his comment on Facebook re the giant Syrian Puppet on B.B.C. news recommending the puppet should stay home!*"

Rona referred the comment to me. "*Simon,*" she wrote. "*Any idea what they are talking about I had a look at your F.B. page and I see a couple of things on neighbourhood watch But I do not know what they are talking about.*"

I sent Rona a link to the news article with my comment. "*What a strange email,*" I wrote. "*I follow B.B.C. News. It has an absurd story about 'The giant puppet walking 5,000 miles to the U.K.' I commented: 'How about the giant puppet stay home with her people.' It's a puppet!*"

Rona then presumably contacted Imogen. Again Rona contacted me. "*She wrote back and said that the comment isn't surprising because of the books that you write,"* wrote Rona, *"head shaking."*

"Yes," I replied, *"they're my books, spinning out of my M.B.A. for the nonfiction or novel writing course for the fiction. It's an interesting link to my Facebook comment, but so be it. I've never written books about puppets! Imogen has taken a lot of interest in my Facebook comment, without commenting herself on Facebook from what I can see. Would she like to read any of my books?"*

"My head is just spinning at who had time to filter through the over 300 comments on the B.B.C. page to then work out who you 'work for' in order to complain," replied Rona. *"Oh well.... noted and we move on from here – I don't see that anything else needs to occur. Thanks for the feedback."*

If Imogen also contacted either of the two companies for which I also worked at the time, one of which she could also have discovered through *Facebook* and both of which she could have discovered through *Linked In*, then those companies did not mention it to me. Before that exchange with Rona, I did not know Imogen. I had never before seen her name, so far as I recalled.

Imogen presumably then contacted someone employing the next dissident she tracked down. We need to understand the people who would punish us. Imogen was not unique.

I could not find Imogen's profile on *Facebook*; she seemed not to have one. I found her on the *Twitter* social media website.

Of the people so eager for their countries to welcome all-comers and so hostile to white people unwelcoming, Imogen was a fascinating character study. A retired Scotswoman, she was probably born soon after World War II, a boomer herself, when war-induced rationing still starved Britain and images of the Holocaust were new.

In April 2019, Imogen retweeted that the City of Edinburgh was hiring a Diversity Officer. Retweeting presumably signified her approval.

Imogen published many photographs of her German shepherd dog Lyra. *"Watching Strictly with Mummy!"* described Lyra in front of a television set in December 2020. In September 2019, Imogen owned a cat Eilidh. In May 2019, Imogen tended to a birdbath.

None of her pictures or writings on *Twitter* or on her personal website indicated that Imogen was married, although in April 2020 she published an old black-and-white photograph of her aged twenty with a young child. In November 2019, she mentioned her son being fifty-two years old. There were no recent pictures of her son or evidence of grandchildren.

Imogen lived near the Skye Bridge in rural Scotland. From her photographs, it seemed an isolated home, out of sight from immigrants she might have never met and out of sight from other people altogether. The rest of Britain could collapse in chaos and conflict, while she walked unaffected with her dog through the woods.

I ceased following *British Broadcasting Corporation News*. Comments on social media might sell some books, but might also bring more aggravation. They would not affect anyone's point of view or otherwise change anything. Only my books might inspire people to think. Some years earlier, I had ceased following *The New York Times* on *Facebook* after copping abuse for challenging the newspaper line.

By the end of September 2021, I was self-censoring my comments on a sponsored *Facebook* page appearing before me, feeling unable to correct nonsensical equating of the Austrian von Trapp family of *Sound of Music* fame to modern-day claimants for refugee status in the West. Reading but feeling I could not comment was frustrating. I fell silent on social media.

I did not contact anyone associated with Imogen. I did not contact her. I did not follow her. This Age of Ideology empowers the smallest and meekest of people to assail and seek to punish with impunity any dissident of whom they become aware, even on the far side of the earth.

If ever she should read this book, Imogen might well be pleased. Any fame she found among like-minded Scots might console her for Rona not terminating my consultancy.

My paternal grandmother's mother was a Neill of the Isle of Barra, in the Outer Hebrides of Scotland. I was a member of the Clan MacNeil Association of Australia.

Like other biological tribalism, biological compatriotism endures. In a rational West, treating race as people of other races do, Imogen would have seen me not as her enemy but as her compatriot. I saw her as my compatriot, which doubtlessly no Syrian did.

Caring for our compatriots, we might care for them more than they care for themselves. They might even hate us for caring about them.

Rather than fighting them, we need to turn them around. We

need to inspire them to stand with us, not against us.

Siding with other races against a person's forebears, compatriots, and descendants is irrational. Only we and some Jews do.

Every attack on Western racism compounds our individualism and isolation. Compatriots siding together, as people of other races and most Jews do, are being rational, even if they disagree about what aids their racial interests.

13. COURAGE AND CONVICTION

Answering our leaders' calls through the first half of the twentieth century, we ventured off to two world wars. There, we fought and died. Through the decades after World War II, we rebelled.

Two generations onward, the calls have changed. We have come again to obey.

Literature used to provoke. Rock music used to rebel. They no longer do.

Losing our connectedness, we lack a people's resilience to resist. Faithfully we reiterate in speech and writing at every opportunity the dictates we hear and see. Together we submit to edicts of the elite we feel too meek to defy. We became domesticated, like household cats and dogs.

The imposition and enforcement of select ideologies led to a lack of belief in anything else. People have interests, memberships, and even identities, but few personal beliefs.

Any beliefs people hold, they lack the willingness to stand by when standing by is awkward. If there is conviction there is conviction in each prevailing ideology, although there is often no conviction in that.

Complying with a decree does not mean people feel conviction for that decree. They simply comply, until the next decree comes along. People comply with that too.

Slavishly following the horde is safe. Agreeing is easier than disagreeing.

Compliance is easy. Conviction is not, if conviction defies presiding authorities or the will of the mob.

Standing up to mobs has always been difficult. Keeping out of their way is hard enough.

Tribespeople might comply with their tribal, ethnic, or religious authorities and nationalists with their national authorities, but for all our claims of defiance, we individuals have become increasingly compliant with any human authorities and with the mob of loud opinion. Family, friends, and strangers all saying the same thing and demanding we say it too can feel overwhelming.

It is in the nature of mobs that mobs are irrational, but vulnerability can make questioning hard. Mobs allow no independence.

People join mobs for the chance to belong, when standing idly by is aloneness. A herd mentality is tribalism, if only for points of view. People following a mob are the mob.

Large numbers of people senselessly concur with the loudest voices around, whatever those voices happen to say. They always have.

In the year 399 Before Christ, Athenians followed the gods that the city of Athens decreed. Essentially for wanting his students to think, Athenian authorities sentenced philosopher Socrates to death.

The communist Soviet Union was similar. The West is becoming so.

The most ruthless of totalitarian dictatorships permit people free speech, but only to say what the regime allows. People can shout their approval of the government and government policy from street corners, but not so much as whisper dissent to their spouses in bed.

We are the same. Our right of free speech is a right to say we agree.

For all our talk of rights, we do not enjoy the rights we once had to speak as we wished. We feel prohibited from protesting that we lack freedom to dissent, because that would allude to secret dissent: that we would dissent if we could, but force instead of righteousness or merit prevails. Thinking and feeling anything we are unfree to reveal becomes difficult.

Bullying became socially acceptable, provided it is of people with whom authorities disagree. It is our ideological tribalism, pitting us against dissenters we become free to bully as bigots as if they were the wrongdoers and lunatics, whatever we cowardly feel. Agreeing with each prevailing ideology lets us join an ideological posse, tirelessly venting our furies upon our ideological prey caught in our ideological cross hairs.

Inspiring abuse rather than rational argument ought to assure dissenters we are right, although being right will not save our noses from being bloodied. It might draw more blood.

Of course, people abusing dissenters believe they are right, but many refuse to debate or even discuss. Truth and reason do not require the force that irrational ideologies require to enforce. Ideas pleasing to people do not demand submission.

Imposing ideology is the antithesis of freedom. Standing up for reality, reason, or morality at odds with prevailing ideologies takes bravery. Telling the truth about anything important takes men and women of courage, as it normally did not through our Age of Enlightenment.

In December 2019, British writer Joanne Rowling was the richest, highest selling, and probably most popular novelist on earth. That did not protect her from politicians, journalists, and others denouncing her for defending Jewish researcher Maya Forstater. "*Dress however you please*," wrote Rowling on the *Twitter* social media website. "*Call yourself whatever you like. Sleep with any consenting adult who'll have you. Live your best life in peace and security. But force women out of their jobs for stating that sex is real?*"

Men and women publicly poured scorn upon Rowling for defending women engaged with reality from being punished for not submitting to men who were not. They called her transphobic.

Other men and women backed Rowling. There was great irony by 2020 when homosexuals who once bullied dissenters into silence with accusations of homophobia found themselves being bullied with accusations of transphobia. Keeping up with our accelerating decline can be difficult.

Engaging with reality when reality refutes an ideology, respecting our race, country, and culture, or being sexually moral, we have come to be accused of carrying phobias that have nothing to do with suffering irrational fears. They have everything to do with holding rational beliefs.

Instead of curling up in frightened balls when bullies accuse us of this-phobia or that-phobia, we should speak up for reason, reality, and morality. Would homosexuals leave their homosexual lifestyles if we called them heterophobes? Would the critics of European colonialism (but not of other races' colonialism) cease if we called them xenophobes?

Inspiring others to think seems nigh on impossible, as it must have seemed to Socrates. We need to try.

From the beginning, mass interracial immigration shut down recognition of reality. It shut down reason.

When British head teacher Ray Honeyford wrote an article

critical of multiculturalism and its impact on British education, published in *The Salisbury Review* magazine in January 1984, immigration advocates did not debate him. They silenced him. Bradford mayor Mohammed Ajeeb called for Honeyford's dismissal.

Philosopher Roger Scruton was editor of *The Salisbury Review*. His 2006 autobiography he titled *Gentle Regrets: Thoughts from a Life*. "*Ray Honeyford was branded as a racist*," wrote Scruton, "*horribly pilloried, and eventually sacked, for saying what everyone now admits to be true*."

People of other races defending and asserting their ethnic interests by denying us facts and reason are being rational, engaging in normal racial struggles. Doing so in our countries, they can expect to be applauded, especially by us.

People of our race shutting down facts and reason that defend our countries, cultures, and civilisation are being irrational. Defending racial and religious diversity has come at the cost of racial and cultural truth. The Holocaust led to the risk of being accused of prejudice paralysing white people.

We need to overcome our paralysis. We need to fob away accusations of our racism as people of other races would fob away accusations of their racism.

Facts, reason, and morality do not cease being facts, reason, or morality because bullies call them bigotry. Good and sensible people are no less good and sensible because bullies call them bigots.

Traditionally, bigotry was by definition irrational. Thus reporting facts, arguing logically, and espousing morality can never be bigotry.

Authorities and their acolytes can silence dissenters. They can ostracise and exile them. They might even gaol them, in the name of diversity, equity, and inclusion, but they cannot make something bad or untrue into something good or true, or make something good or true into something bad or untrue. No punishment can make fact into fiction or fiction into fact, or make morality into immorality or immorality into morality.

We remain as biologically capable of rational thought as our forebears. We simply refuse to reason, regarding anything important.

If we do think rationally, we keep our thoughts to ourselves.

Speaking up and suffering penalty for no useful return would be irrational.

Force does not persuade people of anything. It simply silences them.

Dissenters might then think of other things and forget. They might not. Authorities presume that people agree with them.

Propaganda, laws, and the force of mobs can leave dissenters feeling peculiar, without reassuring voices to hear or words to read. Powerless to dwell on very much more, our compatriots feeling too few in number focus on the small lives they lead and matters of no consequence, except perhaps to their families and friends. They study or work.

Few people are unique. A lot of reasonable people say a lot of reasonable things in private conversations that a lot of other people never hear from anyone.

There may well be other dissenters seeking the same kept silent. We cannot know. They cannot know.

Unaware of other people's private conversations, new generations never learn significant facts. They never learn to reason. We believe ideologies if ideologies are all we read, see, and hear.

There is no point in saying or writing what everybody else says and writes. We need to be willing to disagree.

Dissent brings applause and adoration from people condemned to doing so in silence, anonymously on social media, or in private conversations, frightened of publicly resisting authorities. Supporting dissent would be our forebears if they knew what we were doing. Dissent needs to prevail for the support of our descendants to mean very much.

Our refusal to recognise reality is never crueller or more irrational than it is amidst people suffering and dying. When the people suffering and dying are people for whom we care or should care, our refusal is never more immoral.

Israeli Jews do not tolerate Arabs killing Jews because Arabs accuse Israel of racism for existing and genocide for defending itself. We let our compatriots die rather than be accused of prejudice.

Aided by his brother, Salman Ramadan Abedi murdered twenty-two concert-goers and their parents outside the Ariana Grande concert at the Manchester Arena in May 2017. People refused to heed warnings beforehand about Abedi to save themselves from being accused of racism or so-called Islamophobia.

They too were culpable. So was everyone who had shamed those people out of truth and reason regarding race and religion.

Instead of insisting that race and religion are not related to crime and terror, we should consider rationally the possibilities they are, especially when criminals and terrorists tell us they are. The race or religion motivating them might be theirs, their victims', or both.

Education, discussion, and debate regarding race or religion require freedom for racial or religious criticism, even vilification, whenever the evidence and reason envision it. We vilify our race and religion, after all.

Love and hatred are natural. Both are often irrational, but can still be understandable.

We feel ashamed for our past prejudices, without trying to understand them. Rather than suppressing prejudice or immediately sympathising with the objects of that prejudice, we should investigate its motivations.

Prejudice might point us to facts about races and their cultures. Knowledge can be useful in all our interactions.

Disadvantaging all races or religions when not all races or religions are responsible for wrongdoing is unjust. Instead of restricting everyone to protect people's lives, we might need only to restrict the races or religions from which threats come.

Discrimination can be discernment. Discrimination is rational, righteous, and just whenever the evidence suggests it might safeguard or otherwise assist us, people for whom we care, or people who we are morally bound to protect and assist.

Rejecting out of hand racial, religious, and other discrimination defending people of our race is irrational and immoral. It weakens people of our race through their struggles, tensions, and conflicts with people of other races.

Our forebears defended us. Our descendants will wish we mended and defended us, if we do not.

Aiding most races does not require courage. No one denies them their natures or self-respect.

We of the West are not the only ethnicities denied our countries and identities: our borders and biology. We might be the only ethnicities denied by our own.

Seeking to mend our broken race – to tell the truth and reconnect with our compatriots – we can expect to be mocked as fools. Our own smile sweetly at rapists and murderers from other races, but lambast our compatriots who have committed no wrong, except express affection for our ethnicities and heritages.

Longing for what other races have, we can expect to be reviled as bigots by people of other races asserting their ethnic interests and by our own turned against us. The nastiness and despair that leaves Westerners willing to lose their country, race, and culture moves them to set their spite upon us wanting our inheritances, to even the most modest and humble of degrees.

To suffer that particularly painful vitriol, we need not act upon our desires. We need only reveal them.

Maligning another race but ours would mean risking our friendships with people of that race. Appreciating our race we risk our friendships with people of our race. If our friends presume anything of us while we are silent, they presume our submission.

Friendships dependent upon us neglecting our forebears, compatriots, and descendants are not friendships. They are acquaintanceships. They are worthless. Speaking up for our cultures and ethnicities requires our willingness to sacrifice acquaintanceships we wrongly think are important.

More important can be the jobs, sports team selections, and other livelihoods dependent upon our public concurrence. We might thus do well to protect ourselves with financial reserves, if we can.

Bravery is not acting without fear. Bravery is acting in spite of being afraid, because the task is sufficiently important.

Our ancestors and descendants are important. Our families, ethnicities, and race are important. We are important.

Saving our civilisation, or saving simply our sweet small families and neighbourhoods, we need to find strength. We need to be bold. Some people need to be stronger and bolder than others.

Dutch politician Pim Fortuyn was murdered in 2002 for defending his country, race, and culture, not by someone of another but by someone of his. The price of righteousness is high.

Rational people do not want to be martyrs. Rational heroes and heroines carry out their missions wanting to live, although not at any cost. Like our forebears dying in our defence, and perhaps our descendants dying in theirs, sometimes heroes and heroines find death inescapable.

Ours is not the valour of our forebears who fought and died to save us, or even the valour of our forebears entering alien lands spreading civilisation. It is valour nevertheless.

Our forebears risked more in war than most of us risk to stand up for truth and reason, but what makes the courage required of us feel more daunting was that our forebears' compatriots stood with them. They marched together and cheered each other marching.

We traipse alone. The only people upon whom individuals can rely are themselves.

Confronted with normal racial struggles, tensions, and conflicts, we cannot take comfort from the support of our race, as people of other races can from theirs. We suffer the frailty of our race, ethnicities, and often our families being indifferent or hostile to us.

There is no greater hatred on earth than the hatred meted out upon white people, but there would be less hatred against us if we were not leading it. We will never create communities when the only commonality between people is our suicidal self-contempt and the contempt of us we encourage in others.

14. MORES AND MORALITY

An English gentleman lied only for the sake of a lady's honour; her honour mattered more than his. Chivalry warranted dishonesty that love and romance did not.

Morality expresses right and wrong. Morals govern what people do.

Social mores dictate what is proper and improper. Mores govern what people are seen to do.

Morality gives rise to mores, as do religion, laws, and ideology, for example. Social mores are societal and other pressures among people wanting to make good impressions.

Compliance with mores can conceal any number of feelings or behaviours, including immorality. Morals are much deeper, more fundamental, than mere mores.

Manners, customs, and mores are culture. They can vary over time, characterising particular communities, societies, countries, ethnicities, and races, without necessarily being unique to any. Those widespread enough among a people are cultural norms.

Facts and reason of themselves are generally neither moral nor immoral, neither proper nor improper, unless the facts are people's actions and, some might say, thoughts. Morality and immorality, propriety and impropriety, lie in what people do with facts, including mentioning them.

Traditionally, morality and mores were born of tribalism. Tribespeople took interests in each other and what they thought of each other.

Mores do not require connectedness for people to comply. People have other reasons to make good impressions upon people they encounter.

Morality requires connectedness. For there to be a good greater than individual self-interest, there must be something greater than each individual. When individual and sectional self-interests do not otherwise align, a tribal interest provides a common greater good.

Across primitive tribes, morality proved largely uniform. Morals developed differently where people or their circumstances differed.

Different tribal natures produced different senses of their common good and different religions. Both could produce different morals. Religious teachers and deities decree greater goods for their faithful.

Through the twentieth century, Soviet communism envisaged a collective good embracing racial and religious diversity, but it did not happen. It has never happened. People feeling moral obligation do so only to their tribespeople.

For there to be a common good there must be commonality. For there to be a collective good there must be a collective: a common tribalism.

A tribe's interest is each tribesperson's interest too. Tribespeople have interests in each other.

Morality is mutual responsibility, every tribesperson for every other. The rules for one are essentially the rules for all, perhaps adjusted for a person's particulars. Morality is reciprocal.

For the good of the tribe and tribespeople, tribalism gave rise to moral prohibitions against tribespeople striking, raping, or killing each other. Helping and safeguarding fellow tribespeople is moral. Harming them or exposing them to risks of harm is immoral.

Human nature being tribal and morality flowing naturally from tribalism, morality arose naturally. Even the most primitive tribes without the structures we might call laws had morality, although tribes often came in time to codify morality into laws. Morals are natural law, independent of human authorities.

If morals did not benefit tribespeople, such morals would not have arisen or endured. Morals are the principles by which people care for each other.

The people most likely to care about us, if anybody does, are our relatives. If we do not care about our families, then nobody will.

Caring for our tribespeople means caring not simply for our tribespeople collectively. It means caring for our tribespeople individually too.

To feel moral obligations towards our compatriots, we need to see them as our compatriots. Their care for our ethnicity and race collectively is their care for us individually too.

If we want our compatriots to care about us, we need to care about them. If we do not care about the rest of our race, it is little wonder if the rest of our race does not care about us.

Sympathy is sensitivity to other people's disappointment or suffering. Empathy is feeling at least a little of other people's feelings.

Emotional empathy requires connectedness. The deepest empathy, perhaps our only remaining empathy, is that of loving parents for their children.

Among people who love, morality is born of love. To love our family, ethnicity, and race is to love others of our family, ethnicity, and race. To love others of our family, ethnicity, and race is to love our family, ethnicity, and race.

A time of connectedness with our family, ethnicity, and race was a time of sympathy and empathy. We had friends upon whom we could rely. We were nice.

Being part of a society meant that we cared about that society and thus people in it. Our connectedness brought us morality in our dealings with people as well as confidence in their morality.

Some people were more moral than others, perhaps knowing they should be more moral. When moral people lied, they felt a need to lie. If the need was theirs rather than their relative or compatriot's need, they felt shame for their lying.

Old people are vulnerable to fraud because the strangers they encountered through their youths were their compatriots they could trust. With the coming of diversity and individualism, they encountered people not their compatriots or not feeling they were their compatriots, but still the old people trusted them.

Hatred or contempt might manifest in immorality. More often, immorality lies simply in disconnectedness.

Without connectedness, people lie without cause. They lie without shame. They might not comprehend shame.

There is no sympathy in diversity, no empathy. There is no morality in multiculturalism.

We used to condemn immorality at work and out of it. Having lost our connectedness and self-assuredness, we came to tolerate immorality.

When the moral compete with the immoral, the immoral normally prevail. To survive, the moral become immoral. Morality dies.

Nor is there sympathy, empathy, or morality with individualism. People lacking empathy we used to call psychopaths or sociopaths, until empathy became rare.

Societies produce morality, but individuals have no societies. We lost our morals when we lost our societies.

Individualism and multiculturalism are incompatible with morality, because there is no collective sense from which a greater good flows. There is no connectedness by which people care for each other. Rejecting senses of being tribes and peoples is rejecting the basis of morality.

Tribalism leaves people without moral obligations towards people outside their tribe: their family, ethnicity, and race. Individualism leaves people without moral obligations to anyone.

Without biological connectedness, personal relationships close enough to be essentially tribes of two might produce feelings of connectedness, empathy, and morality between the two. Unfortunately, we assume our acquaintanceships, friendships, and romances are close personal relationships they often are not.

Only mores remain. Mores only matter to people wanting to make good impressions.

With the breakdown of our societies after twentieth-century war, the greater good ceased being objective. Each individual decides what the greater good entails, irrespective of what other people think.

Western morality became subjective. Relativism rejects any collective or absolute morality in favour of each person's personal morality.

Being grounded in reality, morality is fundamentally incompatible with relativism. Relativism allows people to disregard other people's real-world risks and problems, as well as their own.

Morality became meaningless. If it feels good then it is good, however harmful it is.

Individuals all denote themselves moral. They might denote others immoral, but who cares?

Human authorities do not like natural morality because they can enforce it but, unlike law and ideology, human authorities did not dictate it. Tribes did.

Ideology is not morality. Morality depends upon connectedness. Law and ideology depend upon authorities. Mores can come from anywhere.

Ideologies are intrinsically immoral if they disregard reality. They thus disregard the impact of reality upon people.

Western authorities became immoral before the people did. Without a common nationalism, neither people nor authorities care for the other.

Authorities invent and impose ideologies having regard for their individual or sectional interests. They can err in what they believe their interests to be.

Much as they do with realty, human authorities take the role of deities, decreeing the greater good. Ideologies purport to dictate not just what is true, in spite of the facts, but what is moral.

Agreeing with the prevailing ideologies becomes nominally moral, however intrinsically immoral those ideologies are. Disagreeing with the prevailing ideologies becomes ideologically immoral.

Mores become the new morals. The naturally immoral becomes moral. The naturally moral becomes immoral.

We used to be better than that. We no longer are.

Instead of morality, the West in this Age of Ideology, this Age of Individualism, has individual feelings of moral superiority over our forebears and over our compatriots with whom we disagree. Their beliefs might also be other races' beliefs, although we have become unwilling to feel superior to other races.

Morality commands that we honour our forebears, safeguard our compatriots, and defend our descendants. Deriding our forebears, neglecting our compatriots, or disregarding our descendants is immoral.

Siding with people of other races because they are of other races duelling with people of our race is especially immoral. Few actions and beliefs are more demonstrably immoral than satisfying our feelings of sanctimony to the detriment of our relatives and compatriots.

Our racial self-scorn is individual self-righteousness, enabling us to feel better for our sorry small selves, albeit in the most minor and transitory of ways. Self-righteousness is self-centredness, disparaging of others. It is immoral.

Individualism underpins our racial submission. We presume we remain personally unaffected, while our race declines and cultures dissolve. That is immoral.

Christian missionaries and our past empires aside, morality is generally concerned only with fellow tribespeople. Thus people of other races are not interested in what we or other races but theirs do, unless it affects them. Other races do not care that the West has descended into immorality.

Today, it seems that all the other races of the world see their ethnicity or race as morally superior to the West. They are right.

Other races did not used to be morally superior to us, but they have not changed of late to the degree we have changed. They honour their ancestors, safeguard their compatriots, and aid their descendants. Retaining their tribalism, they retain their morality.

To end our neglect of each other, we need to change back. We need to reacquaint with morality.

When morals compel or constrain us, they do so for our compatriots' benefit or for ours. They compel and constrain our compatriots for our benefit or theirs.

Indifference to each other's well-being is immoral. Thus tolerating each other's immorality is immoral. Tolerating behaviours harming people for whom we should care is a vice. Indifference to immorality is indifference to people.

Morality is not oppression, but protection. Oppression of our compatriots is immoral.

Central to morality is honesty: telling the truth to our compatriots, for their sakes. It is in our interests to be honest with them because it is in our interests for them to be honest with us.

If we do not know the truth, then we should say nothing. There is no shame in not knowing.

If we merely suspect something, then we should say we suspect. We should not doubt our words without saying that we doubt them.

We should only promise what we can deliver. If all we can do is try or hope to deliver then we should say so. There is no shame in failing if we try.

People can be honest without morality, when honesty is in their legal, reputational, or other interests. We need to ensure that it is.

Morality means being honest when honesty is not in a person's immediate individual interests. Morality makes honesty instinctive.

Hypocrisy is wrong because of the hypocrite's wrongful act or omission. It is also wrong because of the hypocrite's deceit implying he or she does not commit the wrong.

Without morality, hypocrisy cannot be immoral. Without morality, nothing can be immoral.

Greed is immoral because it denies a person's compatriots what they need or deserve from limited resources. Without a connection to the people denied, greed is not immoral.

Individualism is amorality. Our rich become individually richer at the expense of our poor, selling the West to ruin.

Rich individuals cannot keep their riches when they die. Collectively, their families and ethnicities can, if they share their wealth with their own. Other races do.

Indulging or affirming our compatriots' immorality is not empathy, but apathy. It is selfish and lazy.

Assisting people takes effort, keeping them from harming themselves or our compatriots. It is not automatically agreeing with them but correcting them if need be.

If we believe our compatriots' actions or lifestyles harm them, their families, or our compatriots and they are unaware of that harm, then we should tell them. They should tell us if they believe our actions and lifestyles harm us, our families, or our compatriots.

We and they should feel free to answer. They and we might then debate.

That is how people look after each other. It is how we survive.

Tribespeople want to know their moral obligations. They might not hold fast to those obligations, but they know they should, if only because their fellow tribespeople punish them otherwise.

Societies developed morality in people's interests. Those same interests necessitated societies enforcing morality.

To care, we need to be willing to judge. Judgement is not simply opining or declaring a person or people to have done wrong. Judgement is also imposing punishment, casting stones metaphorically or literally.

Opinions and declarations without punishment are not judgements. We should feel free to opine and declare about anyone and anything. So should our compatriots about us.

For morality to have a place among people, it must have a place in the law. Traditionally, civil and religious authorities enforced moral laws.

If civil and criminal laws do not mandate morality, they should at least allow it. They should not prohibit it.

Traditionally, society's first sentence against immorality was social exclusion. If ostracising the immoral seems harsh, then the ideological West is harsher, expanding upon that exclusion.

Ideology has proven more judgemental than morality ever was.

We judge people for their beliefs with which we disagree.

Societies often forgave people who repented of their immorality, punishing only the unrepentantly immoral. Ideologues have proven unforgiving of people found to have dissented from the prevailing ideology, even when their dissent came from a time before the ideology prevailed. Ideologies forgive not even the dead.

In the name of inclusion of other races, we push away people of our race. In the name of inclusion of the sexually immoral, we push away the sexually moral. Failing to subscribe to ideologies claiming to be inclusion has become cause to exclude people, which is as good an example as any of the illogic to which the West has succumbed.

To understand our collective interests and rights, we might take up for our families, ethnicities, and race the rights we have become so quick to claim for our individual selves. We might claim secure homelands for our ethnicity and race.

Only with our biological connectedness is there a greater good, or any objective good, duty, or honour. To understand our duties to our compatriots, we might take up for our individual selves some of the obligations we have become quick to impose upon our governments, countries, and race. We would aid and protect each other.

Duties are mutual. If we want our families and compatriots to feel duties to us, we need to feel duties to them.

Honour is shared. Instead of believing what suits our individual selves, our race and its reputation be damned, honour commands that we defend our race and ethnicity's reputations from falsehood and unfairness.

Authorities need not impose morality, duty, or honour upon people. They need only free us to reconnect with our own.

Reviving our biological connectedness is reviving our natural tribalism. With our families, ethnicities, and races again, we should again enjoy our common identities. With each there would be a common good, a greater good, releasing our innate shared morality. It will probably take time.

15. SEXUAL MORALITY

There is no more basic a natural instinct than to survive. Survival is not simply individual.

Survival is also genetic. Zebras have our sympathies being eaten alive by lions, but male zebras, lions, and other animals kill newborns of their species they did not sire, replacing them with their offspring.

Survival is also collective, that of the tribe. Tribalism might be the single most important element of human nature. From tribalism, other natural instincts flow.

As every other race on earth but ours still understands, tribal survival requires parenthood. Biological families produce children. Metaphorical families do not produce anything.

Instincts to survive are instincts to reproduce and procreate. Those instincts fall within the field of psychology known as evolutionary psychology.

Sexual morality is one aspect of morality. With one there should be the other. Without one, there has often proven to be neither.

That morality flows naturally from our innate tribalism is most obvious regarding sexual morality. It is well-being and survival, individually and collectively.

Thus tribesmen and women came together in marriage. Polygamy was common in primitive societies, almost always with men taking a number of wives rather than women taking a number of husbands. It remains common in parts of the world. Monogamy or polygamy might be more of a cultural norm than a matter of morality.

Polygamy deems a man most successful by the more wives he has. Monogamy deems a man most successful by the fewer wives he has, provided he has at least one. A successful woman needs only one husband, provided he is a good husband and father.

Social mores often change over time. Morals normally do not.

If morals appear to change, there is a rational underlying reason for change: a change in circumstance. The greater good does not change.

Pre-marital relations were immoral because of the pregnancy risk for women. With contraception, the pregnancy risk diminished. There might thus be reason to allow consensual pre-marital relations.

A pregnancy risk for women remains. The new expression of that moral obligation might be for a man to propose marrying a woman he made pregnant if contraception fails. She can decide whether accepting his proposal is in her and her baby's interests.

Amidst the scars of war and threats of more war through the decades after World War II, families remained the foundations of our communities. Families brought belonging, when too little else that once did still did.

Whatever the traumas of our past, loving spouses can heal us. Whatever the anxieties of the present, loving families can comfort us.

Mutual commitment need not be a burden. It can be a bastion for men, women, and children.

Marriage should provide mutual stability, security, and support. Love and friendship should flourish in marriage.

The well-being of fathers, mothers, and especially children depend upon the well-being of families. Their mutual well-being depends upon each of them, especially the adults, accepting moral obligations towards each other, for the good of each of them individually and of their family.

We need not only to bring our compatriots together in mutually beneficial marriages. We need to help them remain there. With some exceptions such as abuse, disease, infidelity, and infertility, divorce within an ethnicity is immoral.

Adultery is immoral for harming the family and thus family members. Their compatriots object on behalf of those family members and because any spouse flagrantly denying the sanctity of marriage undermines other families.

Aiding a family and ethnicity's survival is moral. Prejudicing a family or ethnicity's survival is immoral.

Repealing moral laws after World War II would not have repealed morality if our societies had been allowed to persist, with societies' judgements against the immoral. Ideologies of inclusion erode morality by denying people the force of social exclusion.

Sexual morality is not bigotry. Morality is rational. Bigotry is irrational.

Like other morality, the premise of sexual morality is tribalism: tribespeople looking after each other. The premise of diversity is individualism: people not caring about others provided they remain personally unaffected.

Abandoning morality is one thing. The West prohibits it.

Western bigotry is bigoted against sexual morality. That is irrational.

For the moral, there is the same recourse as that of other dissidents: holding fast, even if it feels like few of our compatriots do. We do not need to lie if we keep silent, but quietly practice and secretly teach our children morality.

The rest of us can start by applying our talk of tolerance to tolerating morality. If people have a right to preach immorality, then people ought to have a right to preach morality. If people have a right to depravity, then their compatriots have a moral obligation not to deny it is depravity.

We ought not to reject morality without being willing to debate it. The immoral might then learn the benefits to them of morality.

If facts drive men and feelings drive women, then the West has feminised. If women are naturally submissive then that might only be to men they feel care for them, keeping them safe. White men and women have come to fight only each other.

Our collective need to survive makes gender identities, contests, and conflicts mutually destructive. Only monogamous marriage requires an equal representation of genders. Polygamous marriage is better without it.

To reject either gender is to reject our families, ethnicity, and race, upon which the two genders coming together depend for survival. Misogyny and misandry reflect our racial self-rejection, as they do not in other races.

Similarly reflecting our racial self-rejection is our rejection of sexual normalcy, on which ethnic and racial reproduction depend. In her 2020 book *Me, Not You*, British gender-studies academic Alison Phipps wrote that *"white supremacy and heteropatriarchy go hand-in-hand."*

Patriarchy and matriarchy used to be for our collective good. With morality, they can be again.

To observe the overwhelming majority of human relations through history is to see human nature in heterosexual desires.

Recognising sexual norms is thus scientific.

Reason produces the same conclusion. Biological reality and our inherent instinct to survive, our evolutionary psychology, make men and women naturally heterosexual.

Losing our familial, ethnic, and racial self-respect denies us reason to want our families, ethnicities, and race to survive. We lost that impetus for procreation.

Western individualism denies us our families, ethnicities, and races altogether. We have nothing beyond our individual selves to survive.

Recovering our ethnic and genetic self-respect revives our desire for ethnic and genetic survival: childbearing. Heterosexuality is survival.

Rejecting heterosexual norms is rejecting survival. It is rejecting reason and human nature.

To deem every activity and lifestyle morally equivalent is to deny morality altogether. If nothing is immoral, then nothing is moral.

When a glut of people causes crowding, then a race or ethnicity's interest might be in bearing fewer children. Today, some races and ethnicities in that situation. We are not.

Feelings must be free and sincere, but when our feelings move us towards self-neglect, self-degradation, or self-harm, we should not act upon them. With their family, ethnicity, and race in decline, people adopting lifestyles denying them chances to reproduce they would otherwise have are immoral. Discouraging their compatriots from reproducing is also immoral.

Saying love is love is meaningless. Saying anything is itself is meaningless. It does not magically make one feeling the same as another.

Talk of people being cis-heteronormative is ideological wordiness, but through the nonsensical vocabulary is recognition that men and women comfortable in their genders and attracted to each other are normal. Their feelings are natural. Theirs are the only feelings that are.

We used to investigate the causes of unnatural feelings; we used to think. Reason is open to the possibility that people's unnaturalness indicate deeper feelings awry or, at the least, less than ideal.

Good mental health involves people engaging with reality, being rational, and acting naturally. What we used to call perversion or mental illness, we came to call diversity.

Sexual diversity is brokenness. It is unnatural. Authorities would not have to work so hard to normalise abnormal behaviours and lifestyles if those behaviours and lifestyles really were normal.

Understanding unnatural desires helps us to help people. How many people miss out on the contemplation or counselling they need because we celebrate gender and sexual diversity, instead of exploring what confusions, traumas, or yearnings lead people to their aberrant desires?

Ideally, we ease those burdens. We avert them in others.

When unnaturalness becomes as common as it has become in parts of the West, it is symptomatic of something skewed within us. The people we fail to help include us.

Sexualities intrinsically incapable of giving rise to children are self-destructive. People traditionally saw such nihilistic desires as immoral, although they rarely encountered them. Only heterosexuality can bring people into existence, whatever those people's feelings become.

An argument for decriminalising homosexual acts through the second half of the twentieth century was that consensual acts between adults were private. By 2022, nothing was more public around the West than homosexuality.

Bandying about talk of community where there is none, the sense of community we most encourage in white people lie in sexual and gender deviance. Is it any wonder that people want to join? People want to belong.

Personal pride is immoral for being self-absorption, neglecting everyone else, but bringing together two matters most important to the West – money and ideology – the Royal Mint in 2022 issued a colourful fifty pence coin espousing pride. By 2022, talk of pride in the West did not require exposition.

The coin linked pride with protest, unity, visibility, and equality. Protest is purpose and unity is tribalism, but this pride, purpose, and unity was not for Britain. It was personal pride in being anything but heterosexual comfortable with biology.

When we shame our race but exhort pride in something else, is it any wonder if people pursue something else? People pursue pride. For diversity to celebrate us, we cannot be normal.

At the Eryldene house in December 2023, a female university

lecturer (Macquarie University, I think) in behavioural sciences told me that young heterosexual men and women comfortable in their gender, without psychiatric issues, felt like they were "not part of the in-crowd." People like to feel in, to feel they belong.

By Anzac Day 2024, Sydney city buses declared "*You are loved*," but not to Australia's war veterans. The buses were marked with the rainbow colours rejecting sexual normality and biological reality.

Sexual abnormality and gender dysphoria have become rare means by which white people are free to feel pride, loved, and belonging. No race has felt more in need of pride and of feeling loved and belonging than we have by 2025.

If we felt our human nature, we would feel our tribal nature. As people of other races find of theirs, we would find community, unity, and belonging among our families, ethnicity, and race.

Venerating families, we would not venerate diversity. Families and parenthood are the paths to feeling loved, provided we love.

If we were rational, then we would feel pride in our ethnicities and race as people of other races feel pride in theirs, although not so much in our ethnicities and race of late. We would want to reproduce. Rather than feigning pride in perversion, any personal pride we felt would lie in being good spouses and parents.

Where unnaturalness is commonplace, the abnormal become common. To continue attracting attention, to continue to shock and rebel against nature and normality, diversity becomes more and more debauched.

There would be a lot less diversity without attention seeking. There would be a lot less attention seeking without senseless celebration of diversity. Symptoms of our decline exacerbate our decline.

Ideologies are generally concerned only with white people, but a sweeping exception to our obliviousness to what other races do is sexual morality. That other races retain sexual morality does not prompt us to realise that sexual morality is normal and natural. Instead, it moves our authorities to press other races to abandon their sexual morality too, unless pressing those other races affects business.

Our authorities press them with media, money, and marketing. In 2021, American embassies around the world flew most emphatically not the American flag, but the rainbow flag representing sexual diversity.

By 2023, the rainbow flag was becoming ever more complex, trying to encompass everything biologically unreal and sexually unnatural. Another year meant another colour, line, or shape in the flag.

With each aspect of our worsening uniqueness, we should wonder who wants it. It is not us.

People of other races protest against us promoting immorality among them and their children. Immigrants promoting immorality for the West without promoting immorality in their race please their allies among us, but they wish ill upon us.

Not to bear children is to die, in a genetic sense. Wilfully not bearing children is suicide, in a collective sense. Promoting sexual immorality, gender dysphoria, and other childlessness across an ethnicity or race is genocidal.

Instead of espousing sexual diversity to the world, we need to revive sexual normality at home. Connected as we should be to our descendants, determined as best we can be to having descendants, not to care what happens beyond our lifetimes is immoral. To allow, whether wantonly or neglectfully, our family, ethnicity, or race to decline is immoral, whatever our pains or motivation.

Our motivation being money, the applause of other races, or personal self-righteousness is especially immoral. Only a race without morality could allow its demise.

The West's abandonment of sexual morality is a facet of our abandonment of morality in general. Businesses that became amoral in their commercial dealings have become equally indifferent to sexual immorality, unless it affects business.

The same indifference to people that seeks immigration to depress employee wages or boost revenue celebrates sexual behaviours without chance of reproduction. It is indifferent to the gender dysphoric undergoing medical procedures sterilising them, driving our self-destruction.

Enjoying their self-respect, men and women of other races but ours see beauty in their women and handsomeness in their men. Many seem also to see as much of certain races not their own, especially fair, blonde, and blond-haired Europeans. Only we refuse to look so well upon ourselves.

As we understood in our time of self-belief, no women are more beautiful and no men more handsome than those of our ethnicity, when we want to be. Too many of us no longer want to be.

In recent years, Western advertisements, films, and television programmes have come to portray mixed-race couples out of all proportion to their numbers. It can seem that most of the white faces left to see are in relationship with people of other races.

Those relationships are normally incidental background to the primary messages being presented. Subliminally, they legitimise and promote such relationships.

The procreation of a people is procreation of that people, not other people. An ethnicity or race's survival depends not only upon child bearing. It depends upon bearing children of that ethnicity and race. People can have friendships, even relationships, with people of other races, but human instincts for tribalism and survival are to bear children within a person's ethnicity and race.

Our tribal instinct to survive is not just of necessity heterosexual. It is of necessity heterosexual within our ethnicity and race.

Bearing mixed-race children is not ethnic or racial reproduction. It is not racial survival.

Miscegenation need not matter to races already so numerous in the world they do not need more reproduction. We now do. We lose those family lines.

People tend to see mixed-race children as being not of their race. In May 2023, a friend told me of his brother marrying a Japanese woman. The school in Japan at which their child studied segregated Japanese children from other children. Their mixed-race child was among the other children.

Outside the West, mixed-race children are without race. Mixed-tribe children are without tribes. They can be the most solitary of solitary people, not belonging with anyone. That makes mixed-race marriages immoral.

In the West, individualism already leaves us without race, but before the Holocaust, mixed-race child bearing was unusual and often unwanted. Mixed-race offspring were most likely the result of soldiers, slave owners, or other empowered men comforting themselves with conquered, enslaved, or other disempowered women.

Their successors are the men and women comforting themselves with others in need. The disempowered women have become increasingly ours.

Races that care for themselves care especially for their vulnerable: those most in need of protection. Physically, that is their women and children.

Tribesmen and women protect women of their tribe from being raped. They care less about women of other tribes being raped.

The West has become the other way around. British authorities allowed gangs of men to sexually abuse thousands of working-class English girls because the men were immigrants.

In 2021, British-founded confederation of charities Oxfam distributed staff-training slides citing Alison Phipps' 2020 book *Me, Not You*. The slides suggested that white women reporting they had been raped and pressing for criminal charges against their rapists "*legitimates criminal punishment, harming Black and other marginalised people.*"

Phipps criticised whiteness but capitalised black. She denoted white women as privileged, notwithstanding black men raping them. Phipps, a mother, was white.

Reviving our biological connectedness and self-respect would not just provide another reason to bear children. It would be reason to protect our vulnerable.

16. PURPOSE

Much of our self-destructive self-indulgence arises from having nothing useful to do. No longer are most of us striving to eat, drink, and have shelter. Effortlessly, we are nourished and dry. Within our homes, we are cool or warm largely as we wish.

While our forebears depended primarily upon their family, friends, and communities for entertainment, we have endless avenues to be entertained alone, but in the hollows of our minds, we are ultimately bored. Our individual, isolated lives have proven to be without purpose to pursue.

To live, we must want to live. To survive, we must want to survive.

The measure of a purpose is the value it gives a life, not only through a life but nearing life's end, gazing back. A life lived purposefully might still have regrets, but those regrets are minor and few aside the satisfaction of a purpose fulfilled.

The best purposes offer endless fulfilment. If purposes are finally fulfilled, people need new purposes. It is what old people mean by wanting to feel useful, especially old men while their wives tend to their grandchildren.

Purposes unfulfilled are better than no purposes, but contentment lies less in objectives than in outcomes. Contentment lies not in what people want to do or think and feel they do, but in what they actually do and thus know afterwards they have done, without deceiving themselves or others. Purpose is real or not at all.

Victimhood is the antithesis of purpose. Purpose is premised upon personal responsibility to achieve something. Victimhood evades personal responsibility to excuse not achieving something.

Being a victim of wrongdoing or misadventure or even of many wrongdoings and misadventures need not lead a person to retreat into a perpetual feeling of victimhood. For irrational victimhood to become rational relies upon the privilege we have increasingly given victims and people claiming to be victims since the Holocaust.

Through our two world wars and other wars, victims really were victims. For the Jews who died through the Holocaust, we felt guilty.

From the Holocaust came our love affair with victimhood, but physical, economic, and political victimhood gave way to ideologically ordained victimhood. The worst of all victimhood is that claimed by people who are not victims of anything, fortunate as they are, but who claim to be victims.

Purpose requires strength of character. Victimhood is a weakness of character.

Instead of attention, we need achievement, whatever that achievement. Attention is no less superficial and transient when people call it fame.

Achievement is substantial. It might endure, albeit in anonymity.

Fame fades, as we realise getting older. The deaths of people once famous pass by barely noticed. Saying that a deceased relative or friend will never be forgotten might momentarily console us, but he or she will be forgotten. People do not live forever in our hearts, not least because our hearts do not live forever.

Infamy fades faster than the aspiringly infamous imagine. People forget quickly the names and faces they want to forget.

No person feeling that his or her life has purpose would die wantonly or by wilful neglect. No race or ethnicity would.

Supporting a sporting team is not a purpose, however passionate that support. It is spectating. Playing sport is exercise. Both are leisure.

Dining is not a purpose, whatever the restaurant and cuisine, whoever the chef. It is eating. Beer, wine, and spirits are not a purpose, whatever the brewery, winery, or distillery. They are drinking. Eating and drinking are sustenance, however pleasurable.

With purpose, we need not purchase more goods and services in an insatiable pursuit of happiness. Shopping should be incidental to the rest of our lives. It is a necessity to make as pleasant as can be, but purchasing is still not a purpose.

Beliefs are not purposes, although they can provide a framework by which people find purpose, if they are grounded in reality. Purpose is grounded in reality.

Feelings of purpose grounded in something unreal, however real it seems, are not a purpose. They lack achievements. Illusory purposes distract people from real purpose.

A career is not a purpose. It is work, which should be as enjoyable and rewarding as each person can find it. Providing money and thus shelter and sustenance, work can be a means of pursuing purpose through work or outside it.

Purposes need to be natural, or they are more pursuits dictated by schools and other authorities. Without connectedness to the people they influence and so care for those people, governments and businesses promote lifestyles, beliefs, and behaviours they think suit their political or monetary interests, but do not necessarily suit the people affected.

Traditionally, primarily men provided materially for their families, as their capacities allowed. Women bore and nurtured their children and thus their families and people, as their capacities allowed. Among their respective chores, primarily women carried out the family shopping and then some, if the family could afford it.

Since late in the twentieth century, business interests have convinced us that spending and careers are intrinsically important for their own sakes. They feminised men to purchase and masculinised women to labour for money beyond their familial necessities.

What social benefit is there in pushing men and women, most ubiquitously women, into vocations? Men and women work to support themselves and their families when somebody must: a means to an end. There is nothing intrinsically important to work.

Employers and employees are dispensable. So are suppliers and customers, lawyers and clients, voters and candidates.

Focusing our lives upon careers and consumption is unnatural, although they can contribute to lives lived naturally. If they fulfilled people within, then authorities would not need to strive so hard to promote them: to market them.

Feeling part of a people provides purpose. For people of races other than ours, whatever their religion or country of residence, their families, ethnicities, and race are often their purpose. They better them in their countries and elsewhere, through work, business, and welfare, and in government, committees, and community activities. We respect and award them for doing so.

Purpose can lead our minds beyond our individual selves into something bigger and worthwhile, but the causes now consuming us are distant from us: other people's causes or abstract causes not for people at all. When we think people from whom we are separated are our purpose, our purpose is charity.

Without connectedness and the reciprocity it provides, our charity for other races is our white man's burden. It means less to other races than it means to us, but we need something bigger than our individual selves in which to believe.

People are a substantive purpose when biological connectedness provides the benefactor a common identity. Connectedness begins with families: our primary units bigger than mere individuals. Thus people begin with families. There is no more profound a purpose in life for a person than his or her family.

American-born actor Matthew Perry's parents separated when he was a year old, although he went onto an unusually good relationship with his stepfather. Perry prayed for fame and attained it, along with popularity and fortune, but struggled through years of substance abuse. He had many romantic relationships but never married or fathered a child, drowning in his millionaire's hot tub in 2023, aged fifty-four.

Friends said afterwards that for years, all Perry had wanted was to be a husband and father. He made a sad mess of going about it.

The people who tell us we should be alone are mistaken, if not lying. Other people's aloneness might console them through their pains and trials, trying not to feel so alone.

Human nature provides purpose that human authorities cannot. Lives lived naturally are men courting women. They are women courting men or subtly attracting the men they want courting them.

The attention worth attracting is the attention people are not obviously trying to attract. People who naturally lure need not flaunt or boast.

They need only be sensible and genuine. Their clothes and adornments should complement their natural selves.

Men and women recognising their handsomeness and beauty do not vandalise their bodies. The only colours bodies need are natural. Staining or piercing our skin defiles us.

Abnormalities aside perhaps, no surgeon, implant, or injection improves upon nature. Authenticity is attractive. Lies are not.

With lives lived naturally, men would compete with other men not for promotions, but to court women. Women would undermine other women not to aid their careers, but in their competition for men.

Men and women might study, work, earn their reputations, or seek political power to aid them through those competitions, and in time to provide for and safeguard their families. At some point, perhaps immediately, men woo the women they want bearing their children. Women flirt with the men they want fathering their children.

All a man's girlfriends and all a woman's boyfriends are important, as are those who never quite were. The most important is ideally the current, becoming the last, with whom he or she bears children.

Their courtships successful, human nature is then men and women creating people together. To families and thus to clans, ethnicities, and races, parents are indispensable. So are children.

Aside from issues of immediate life and death, fulfilling our instincts to procreate cater to our quality of life more profoundly than anything else we do. The world would be calmer and people more secure if husbands and wives shared more time together, with their children.

Courtship matters more than career. Choosing the person we marry is more important than choosing a university course. Bearing and raising children is more important than rising through a profession.

That men and women have come to imagine their careers being more important than flirting with and wooing each other says much of how far we have fallen from nature. No matter the motivations, advocating work and consumption beyond their necessities risks them coming at the expense of parenthood.

A man can have no greater mortal purpose than pleasing his wife. A woman can have no greater mortal purpose than pleasing her husband.

To that end, they provide for the other and their children as their respective capacities allow. They raise their children well.

Marriage and parenthood measure men and women's success more profoundly than anything else we do. They are essential to life: a central purpose of being. Most races but ours still understand that.

In April 2025, the Tokyo Metropolitan Government introduced a four-day working week. It wanted Japanese to bear children.

Friends often pass through. Parents should not.

Children have many opportunities for friends. They have at most two opportunities for parents.

Parenting is not friendship. Parenting teaches and guides, as best as each parent can. Parenting sets boundaries and rules for each growing child's sake.

Defending and asserting each child's well-being, parenting is strong. It defies the dictates of others if the family's interests require it. Parental resilience teaches children and the adults they become to be resilient.

The only people who need know what parents are doing and have done are their families. To their children, parents are everything, as much in their strengths as their failings.

Purpose lies not only in bearing children but in raising them secure with their place in the world. Their place in the world depends upon their places in their family, ethnicity, and race and upon the places of their family, ethnicity, and race in the world.

Security in their places requires some degree of individual, familial, ethnic, and racial self-respect. More important even than us recovering our racial self-respect is us providing self-respect to our children. Our racial pains and irrational lack of racial self-confidence are hereditary if we let them.

Reason teaches reason: teaching children to think. Rational parenting demands regard for reality: teaching children the truth.

All our children need to enjoy racial self-respect is the truth. Leaving generations to be misled if we can correct them would be immoral.

Childhood fantasies need not harm children, provided we tell them the truth along their paths into adulthood. Lying to children about matters perpetually frightening them, diminishing their self-esteem, or otherwise harming them is child abuse. Child abuse continuing to harm children into adulthood is adult abuse.

Generations of our children are being increasingly misled about matters of the utmost importance. If they are not being lied to, they are being misled by people who have also been misled. Somewhere beyond what might have been a long chain of unwitting errors, somebody blundered or lied.

The falsehoods our children are fed about race instil in them our self-loathing. The falsehoods they are fed about gender and sexuality corrupt them.

If we do not allow our children confidence in their ethnicity, race, and heritage, then they will look to people with confidence in theirs. They will seek purpose where there is self-assuredness, however misplaced that self-assuredness might be.

Whether headed to other races, their religions, or ideology, our children denied their racial self-respect might well turn on their race. If we hold our race in contempt, is there any wonder if our children do too, even if the paths they take are more extreme than our paths have been? They become the ideological, religious, and other warriors hating us, hating them.

Their warfare might be metaphorical. It might be literal.

Healthy parenting nurtures children to become healthy adults, whatever their trials or adversity. Their self-respect enables them to marry, bear children, and raise their children confident in their place in the world. Their parents' purpose fulfilled becomes their purpose fulfilled.

The debt we owe our parents and other forebears we repay by providing for our children, wanting better lives for each succeeding generation, as our ancestors wanted for us and as people of other races want for their children. With descendants, we have lives beyond our own.

We have most importantly, and most challengingly, reason to contemplate the future beyond our relatively short lives on earth. We should do so not with wide-eyed optimism and trust in the benevolence of other races, but rationally according to the evidence.

Prediction is difficult, but we can look to the reality we know. The present is more important than the past, but only by knowing the past can we make sense of the present. Only the future is more important than the present, but only by knowing and understanding the present and past can we provide as best we can for the future.

The past cannot change. The present can change, to a point. The future is most open to change. Purpose focuses upon the future, when that purpose has or has not been fulfilled.

Instead of running away from bad things, we should live our lives seeking good things, like survival, sustainability, and prosperity. Our minds are more peaceful and thoughts happier when we dwell upon what we love and desire instead of what we hate or fear.

That is most notably regarding us. We should love life more than we fear death.

Environmental sustainability is conservation. Returning to reality and reason with self-belief is to resume caring for our natural environment because we care for ourselves, with confidence in our ability to answer challenges. We should want to survive to continue enjoying the flora and fauna, the water and air, as we used to do.

In nature, there is subtlety, the like of which human artwork might match but has not surpassed. There is elegance, splendour, and intricacy in nature no human handiwork can reach.

Nature is beautiful. It can also be brutal.

Lion cubs cutely amble along trails with their mothers, but eat impala calves alive. Young leopards toying with baby gazelles eat those gazelles when they become hungry.

There are no rules between species. There are few rules within them.

If we can revive our naturalness, much will change. Human beings are omnivorous. People might not like the taste of meat or animal products. They might practice religious discipline or hold beliefs about health dissuading them from eating meat.

There should be no vegetarianism or veganism on ideological grounds. Imagining that humans should not eat animals is absurd. Animals eat animals.

Nature includes human beings. It includes us, in our wondrous forms.

People caring for nature and the natural environment save not only bald eagles from extinction. They save their family, ethnicity, and race.

Instead of fretting about the seasons getting warmer decades after our deaths, we should worry about our descendants not seeing any seasons. We should worry about not having descendants.

Individuals die. Families, ethnicities, and races need not die.

With connectedness, we have families to further, ethnicities to evolve, and a race to progress. We have countries to keep and a civilisation to sustain.

Wanting our families, ethnicities, and race to survive and prosper is natural and rational. Anything else is unnatural and irrational.

If our families survive, our ethnicities and race survive, the West survives. Our cultures and civilisation survive, whatever our cultures and civilisation happen to be.

We need life, not death, to revel in our people and cultures. We should strive to survive, with gratitude to our forebears and expectations of our descendants' gratitude to us.

17. MENDING WESTERN CULTURES

The basic natural mechanics of life include eating, drinking, and mating. Cultures are everything that people think, feel, and do beyond those mechanics, including any characteristics by which people carry out those mechanics.

Plainly, people do not all think, feel, and act uniquely. Commonalties generally in a people's beliefs, attitudes, and behaviours are that people's culture.

Cultures need not be unique to a people. They do need to be less than universal. Anything eternally universal might be human nature, mechanics of life, or morality, if we still had morality.

People of other races retain their racial, ethnic, and other tribal connectedness. Thus they inherit from their forebears, share with their contemporaries, and bequeath to their descendants their racial, ethnic, or other tribal cultures, even if they personally do not participate. Their collective self-respect makes them comfortable doing so.

The Middle East, Far East, and so forth are not just those ethnicities and countries but also their cultures. The West is not just European ethnicities and countries, wherever our countries happen to be, but also our cultures.

Much is common in each. None are completely uniform.

Scottish Lowland culture differs from Scottish Highland culture. The differences can seem more pronounced to Scots than they seem from outside.

Individuals might or might not adopt their ethnicity's styles, tastes, and designs. Fine arts contribute to a culture when compatriots claim artists' work for their ethnicity.

Commonalties in cultural and social organisation make for a civilisation. Traditionally, we required civilisations to have at least a degree of technology, in the context of their era. Through the decades following World War II, having lost faith in our civilisation, we relaxed that requirement, at least informally. Colonial Europeans especially came to treat indigenous peoples as at least as civilised as we were.

Western individualism denies us our connectedness. Thus it denies us our inherited and contemporary cultures. We inherit cultures anyway.

Without a tribal connection, culture is each individual's alone, however common it is at a place and time. Cultures common by mimicry, selection, dictation, or chance, such as corporate cultures, tend to be trite.

From attitudes to races come attitudes to their cultures and civilisations. From our past confidence in our race came our past confidence in our cultures and civilisation. From our disillusionment with our race arose our disillusionment with our cultures and civilisation.

Seeing only world wars and the Holocaust, we came to presume our cultures were inferior to others, or that we had no cultures. Neither was true.

Reviving our racial self-respect would refresh our cultural self-respect. Conversely, refreshing our cultural self-respect would revive our racial self-respect. Respect for ourselves is respect for our cultures and civilisation, at least as they were and at least in part.

Ranking cultures varies from time to time. Civilisations rise and fall. Analyses and comparisons ought to be matters for scholarship, not feelings or ideologies, although we should not fault people for feeling good about their race, culture, and civilisation. We used to feel good about ours.

People of other races do not need to characterise their cultures to value them. They simply value them. Valuing their ethnicity and race they value their cultures, whatever their personal practices and beliefs happen to be.

However our wounded Western Civilisation and cultures rank, they are ours. We have reason to repair them.

Mending our ethnicity and race mends our cultures. Mending Western cultures does not depend upon us recognising that we have cultures, although that would help. It depends upon us mending us.

To recognise our cultures and cultural heritage, we need to recognise our connectedness: our race, ethnicity, and pockets thereof. We might then consider what our cultures were and are. Knowing our cultures gives us a chance to appreciate them.

Through much of our histories, Western cultures were cultures of quality, innovation, and diligence, of creativity and imagination. Through our Age of Enlightenment, we enjoyed cultures of individuality.

Ours were cultures of courtesy we conferred upon each other and upon other races. Losing our tribalism, we have become increasingly terse and rude with each other. We nevertheless remain courteous to other races, to the point of submission.

No longer do we expect expertise and even competence in many of the services we receive. Politely we accepted those services declining.

Some people dismiss preference for quality or cleanliness, for civility, civic order, or security, or for anything else better about our cities and countries before other races came, as white supremacy. That says much of the countries we used to enjoy. It also says much of other races.

Self-respecting races assert their cultures wherever they can: in their countries and in ours. Fearing them feeling excluded, we also assert their cultures in our countries.

Our ideology of inclusion is not really inclusion, because we exclude each other and our cultures. Ideologies of diversity seek only our omission. Multiculturalism is any cultural experience but ours, however culturally homogenous it is. Proudly, we neglect and erase any vestiges of our cultures.

We subject ourselves to irrational contradictions. We are supposed neither to practice our cultures nor to appropriate other races' cultures. Both might offend people of other races.

We let people of other races dictate to us what we can wear, write, and do of their cultures, while we refuse to ask anything of them. We offer them our inheritances if they want them, without maintaining our inheritances for us.

Freely adopting another race's culture is a compliment to that race. Imposing other races' cultures upon us, or denying us our cultures, is oppression.

If other races can do as they wish, then surely we can too. Other races choosing their cultures or ours should not impede us from choosing our cultures or theirs.

We ought not to cower from asserting our cultures any more than other races cower from asserting theirs. For our cultures to survive in the face of other races asserting their cultures, we must defend and assert ours in our countries.

We should no more care about our cultures offending other races than they would care about their cultures offending us or each other. Post Holocaust, we treat Western cultures and civilisation as innately racist and racism as wrong, but all races' cultures and civilisations are innately racist because they are races' cultures and civilisations. Races have cultures and often civilisations.

People want culture. People want something more than the mechanics of life.

Without self-respect, that leaves us willing and eager to become subject to other races' cultures because they are other races' cultures. Our confidence in other races is our confidence in their cultures, whatever their cultures happen to be. We embrace what subsumes us.

Multiculturalism, inclusion, and diversity as we understand them all express our lack of racial and cultural self-respect. Only Western countries have taken them up.

Dictates of equality and sameness are not consequences of knowledge. They shut us away from knowledge.

Culture matters more than ideology. Rather than blindly insisting that all cultures, except ours, are equally worthy of respect, rational people only respect cultures and beliefs worthy of respect. To any discerning person and to people of races other than ours, all cultures are not equal.

All cultures are not the same. They might never have been.

Rational people examine the reality of cultures, not just their commonalities but their differences. Cultures differ.

Religions differ. The same religion often differs between races.

In practice and devotion, the same religion often differs between genders. Perhaps more so than men, women generally maintain their ethnicity's mores and other culture. God's police, women enforced their ethnicity's morals.

Human nature appears to include living with some form of religion. There has been religion for as long as people have sought knowledge and understanding of the universe. The West's rejection of religion is our rejection of such knowledge and understanding.

Religions are much deeper, more inspiring, and much more enduring than mere ideology. Indeed, religion defies rule by ideology. Granting authority to a deity, deities, or long-dead human teacher regulates the rule of current human authorities.

Culture includes more than religion, but religion is culture's centre. Religion reflects and affects an ethnicity's understanding of people.

With religion comes more culture. Without religion, culture becomes hollow.

Western Christianity includes carols and hymns to sing, hear, and craft, if we can. It includes Renaissance and other Christian art.

Religious heritages and cultural trappings pervade people's lives more than many of us still realise. Races other than ours, some more than others, want their religion to pervade.

Ideology pervades every aspect of our lives irrespective of whether we want it to pervade. Meanwhile, we compartmentalise religion into a cupboard away from everything else.

People matter more than religion. God matters most of all.

People's most meaningful purposes have proven to be the same two forces, along with human nature, that traditionally most affected human behaviour, generally for the better: gods and tribes. The gods need not be real, although it helps that He is.

For the individualist West, religion is personal: an individual's religion alone, however common or rare the religion. Everything is personal.

Among races other than ours, religion is collective because people are collective. Like race and ethnicity, religions unite people.

Collective religion provides belonging. Personal religion leaves people alone.

A collective religion separates its adherents from other religions. Personal religion separates each adherent from everyone, including everyone else of the same religion.

Much as races and ethnicities have cultures, races and ethnicities have religions. Race being inextricably linked with religion and other culture, ethnic identities bring religious identities.

For the fortunate, their ethnic and religious identities coincide. Their belongings coincide.

Some religions are essentially unique to an ethnicity or race. Other religions several races or ethnicities share.

We no longer let Christianity unite us any more than we let race unite us, but there is English Christianity because there is England and so English culture, including religion. There are countries, cultures, and thus Christianity throughout Europe and wherever

Europeans went. Recognising our Christian heritage and our collective Western identity is recognising Christendom.

People of races other than ours maintain the religion of their ethnicity or race because it is the religion of their ethnicity or race, irrespective of their personal beliefs. People, especially the young, might drift away from their religion, religious rituals, and rest of their cultural heritage, while still owning them.

We could be the same. Instead, our lack of connectedness and collective self-respect makes us uniquely hostile to our cultural heritage.

Self-respect requires us to possess and assess fairly our cultural heritage and civilisation. It does not require us to stagnate or to keep what no longer suits.

Western cultures need not be past cultures or current cultures. They need only be our cultures. We should retain or revive what we want to retain or revive of our cultures, as other races do of their cultures.

Self-respect invites us to develop our cultures and civilisation as reason dictates. We should want always to improve, as we did until the Great War. We would not abandon our heritage because we abandon our forebears, but because our forebears until the Great War also expected civilisation to get better and better the longer we survived.

In particular, self-respect requires us to possess our religious heritage. It does not require us to retain our forebears' religious beliefs. We can embrace our Christian heritage because it is our heritage without holding Christian faith, much as we can embrace our pre-Christian pagan heritage without being pagan.

Like everything else, religion ought to be rational and reflect reality. If reason were to take us back to our pagan religions, then we should return to our pagan religions.

Truth brought European ethnicities to Christianity. We remained Christian throughout our Age of Enlightenment.

The Church is not God. English philosopher Thomas Paine's 1794, 1795, and 1807 work *The Age of Reason* rejected the Church for being self-serving but did not reject Christianity. Rationally observing the natural world, Paine concluded there is a god of some form.

God is no more preposterous than no god. Time and existence are preposterous without ancestors or God.

Our tragic loss of cultural self-belief is nowhere more evident than it is regarding religion. Christians questioning their faith and rationally examining the evidence thereof normally retain Christian faith, but nowhere is our disinterest in truth and reason more in evidence than it is regarding religion.

We claim a commitment to reason and reality when we reject Christianity that we do not cite regarding other religions and beliefs. Rationally examining most of the religions, spiritualties, and mysticism newly in practice around the West since we lost our Christian conviction would quickly dismiss most of them. Those not quickly dismissed would be dismissed soon enough.

Reason rejects superstition. So does religion.

The West re-engaging with reality and reason should re-engage with Christianity. Ideology keeping us from reality and reason keeps us from our religious and rest of our cultural self-respect, keeping us from Christianity.

To remember how good and great a people we can be, we should remember not the hell of a world twice at war but the heaven of Christmas, 1914. Britons and Germans singing 'Silent Night', '*Stille Nacht, heilige Nacht*', together in the cold and dark would have ended that four-year first bloody suicide that night.

Language should not simply be factual. It should be evocative.

The first Renaissance arose through Christian Europe re-reading the writings of classical Greece and Rome. So might the next.

Our classic fine arts represented our bliss in being alive, our senses of awe and wonder. God and our race inspired us. Reviving our cultural self-respect should revive those inspirations.

Conversely, again valuing quality and excellence should revive our cultural self-respect, gazing back upon the richness of our cultural, artistic, and other inheritances. Appreciating our scientific, engineering, and other achievements invites us to achieve more.

Nothing of late has surpassed our classic artwork, music, and literature, although the rare best of each has rivalled it. If our fine arts and culture are again to be great, we need again to judge.

Englishwoman Millie Brown vomiting was not art. It was vomit.

We need to turn away from poor work. We need to discard it.

Gearing arts and culture towards political purposes is a problem when those purposes are self-destructive. Relieving us of our irrational guilt and self-disbelief should wash away those stains upon our perceptions.

Turning from equality back to excellence produces purpose in what we do, and who we are. It invites us to defend and advance our cultures, as people of other races do of theirs.

Through the second decade of the twenty-first century, Hungarians recovering their self-respect began restoring the beauty of Budapest: their architectural heritage. They built elegant facades concealing the stark globalism of their communist-era architecture, such as the blight upon *Kossuth Lajos Tér*: Parliament Square.

Again revering our race and cultures is again revering beauty and intellect. It is revering grace and grandeur over garishness and size.

Beauty and intellect are compatible. In our Age of Enlightenment, they were coincident. Beauty is excellence.

Ideas endure for as long as people believe them. Cultures endure for as long as ethnicities practicing them endure.

Were we to revive our connectedness and collective self-respect as other races retain theirs, we too would be conscious of our cultures. We too would recognise our cultural affinity with others of our ethnicity and race.

Self-respecting people wed someone sharing their culture, willing to share their culture, or letting them practice their culture and pass their culture to their children. They marry someone of their culture or someone without culture.

Thus self-respecting people marrying self-respecting people naturally marry within their cultures, conveying unequivocally single cultural inheritances to their children. Culturally coherent marriages, sharing single cultures, are generally more enduring, with less complication, than other marriages.

18. MENDING WESTERN CHURCHES

Much as companies reflect the countries outside, so do religious bodies. Everything to say of Western countries we can say of Western churches. Church-goers are people too.

From its inception, reality underpinned Western Christianity. Throughout our Age of Enlightenment, so did reason.

So did Christianity. Love rejoices in the truth, wrote the Apostle Paul in his First Epistle to the Corinthians, chapter 13, verse 6.

Anti-Semitism abounded. German priest Martin Luther, the founder of Protestantism, wrote *Von den Jüden und ihren lügen* (*On the Jews and Their Lies*) in 1543.

Debates fail between people making contradictory assumptions. Thus debates fail between devotees of different religions, however rational both devotees are. The Enlightenment failed to overcome diversity.

Europe and her colonies shared our religion with other races because we knew our religion was true. We knew Christianity would help and save other races the world over, because it helped and saved us.

Reverend Edward Owen of the Church of England was rector at All Saints' Church in Hunters Hill, Sydney, from 1900 to 1925, officially to 1926. A century later, two days before Anzac Day in April 2023, the Sunday sermon quoted Owen's diaries. Two-thirds of the men at the church set off to the Great War, wrote Owen, decimating the congregation overnight. A third never returned. Those that returned were broken.

Owen's duties included informing local families of their husbands, sons, and brothers killed in war. Showing people around the church the first Saturday in March 2024, the current reverend said Owen's diaries revealed the Great War broke Owen too.

Charles Raymond Pax George was born in Killara the twenty-sixth day of November 1940, shortly after his father set off to World War II. His parents gave him the name Pax because, in the words of his uncle, a Church of England high church minister at a church near Redfern (not Christ Church St Laurence), baptising him, "What the young child needs in his life is peace."

Charles's widow quoted those words to me at our parish church early in 2024. Pax is Latin for peace.

By July 2023, all thought of Britain and the grace of Empire had gone. "*We meet together on the land of the Wallumata People*," declared the All Saints' Church service of Holy Communion. "*We recognise their connection and custodianship of this land and honour elders past, present and emerging. We lament the past and any hurt and pain caused to First Nations People, especially by the church.*"

Any number of churches around the broken West could have uttered those words, without reason, scholarship, or self-respect. They were lamentations of a broken people inside a broken church, consumed with presumptions about other people's pain but unwilling to understand our pain.

"*We long to be a reconciled people in this land: Lead us on then, Holy Spirit, as we gather from the four corners of the earth; enable us to walk together in trust from the hurt and shame of the past…*"

The problem with Western Christianity as it has come to be is not Christianity. It is the West as the West has come to be.

Being driven so much by feelings, white Christians call those feelings the Holy Spirit, but the Holy Spirit is rational. God is rational. God has self-belief.

For God to mend and fill us, we need to let Him. We need to invite Him. We need to want to be healed.

We don't need to feel worthy to be healed. No one is worthy.

What we need is Christian conviction: belief in Him as the risen Son of God, not simply a nice fellow with some ideas we like. If we want others to believe, we need to believe.

Christian faith has two facets. The first, for those who need it, is the faith that leads a person from believing that Jesus Christ was possibly or probably the Son of God to conviction that He is the Son of God. The strength of that probability and any degree of doubt is for each person to decide. The final step of faith to Christian conviction is emboldening.

The second facet of faith is confidence not simply that God is real, but that He loves us. It is the love that led Him to give His Son to die for us in spite of us being unworthy. Three days later, His Son rose from the dead.

Both facets can wane through times of despair. Through the

first half of the twentieth century, we suffered inconsolable despair.

Both facets can revive through times of joy. Seeing the intricacies of life and feeling the richness, wonder, and splendour of earthly nature is sensing God's joy. Our lives have become estranged from nature, within us and without.

Without tribalism or other felt connection to the people who founded, grew, and sustained a church, the church becomes merely a metaphor. Without devotion to God, the self-appointed faithful masquerade as Christian.

Clergy become the same self-serving sectional interests as other human authorities. Their only difference is that clergy claim at least a passing interest in Christianity.

It is not simply that rich and powerful people around the West lost confidence in their race, culture, and civilisation, and thus confidence in Christianity. It is that those elite still rule Western churches. Even those retaining kernels of Christian faith imagine doing so without regard for their race, country, and rest of their culture, and so with limited regard for God.

At the centre of Western Christianity, the Holocaust replaced the Crucifixion. Jews replaced Jesus.

We made Jesus a Jew, as the Romans did when He walked the earth but as He never did and as we had never before done. Instead of ancient Galilee, He became a Jew in Nazi-occupied Europe. Christ died in Bergen-Belsen and every camp like it, without resurrection.

For the post-Holocaust West, Jewish blood is on our hands. Thus Jesus's blood is on our hands, inverting chapter 27, verses 24 and 25 of the Gospel of Matthew. No longer saving us, Christ in our Holocaust-burnt minds curses the Christian West.

Notwithstanding those words in the Gospel of Matthew, the Apostle Paul in chapter 10, verse 1 of his Epistle to the Romans wrote of "*my heart's desire and prayer to God for the Israelites is that they may be saved.*" He would now write the same of us.

The Holocaust was a matter of race rather than religion, but religion and religious identity came with race. Much as we came to blame ourselves for normal racial struggles, tension, and conflict, we came to blame ourselves for normal religious struggles, tension, and conflict.

Scarred by the Holocaust, secular Western authorities condemn our forebears noting they were white, unconcerned by what other races did. Western clergy condemn our forebears noting they were Christian, unconcerned by what other religions did.

Much like other Western authorities without faith in God or us, Western churches found faith in other races, whatever those other races' religion. Racial diversity and inclusion are a rejection of the West. Religious diversity and inclusion are a rejection of Christianity. Sexual diversity and inclusion are a rejection of everything.

Falsity in church or anywhere else undermines adjoining words of truth. Among the prayers at the Blessed Sacrament Church in Mosman for Epiphany in January 2025 was "that cultural and ethnic diversity shall be appreciated as a source of strength and harmony."

This was not prayer. It was indoctrination, worse than other indoctrination for exploiting the vulnerability of prayer.

It was not praying to God but preying upon people. Cultural and ethnic diversity was not a source of strength and harmony, not even in churches with growing numbers of immigrants.

Scholarship ought to exorcise current heresies because scholarship did not give rise to them. War and holocaust did.

Relativism infected Western churches, erasing two thousand years of Christian knowledge. Ideology replaced Scripture.

Scripture is the word of God, albeit often through human beings. Ideology is the word of human beings, and often single human beings.

God did not invent ideology. People did.

If Christ appeared today or otherwise made Christianity inescapably true, then believing in Him should be obvious, but not in a West without reverence for reality: objective reality. God becomes simply His reality, His identity, while the multiculturalists all go to hell.

There is no more a multitude of religious realities than a multitude of other realities. Whether Jesus Christ is the Son of God is not merely a matter of personal belief. It is a matter of objective fact. No reality is of more consequence than that providing a path to Salvation.

To value our race and ethnicity, we do not need Christian faith. Christian faith should mean we value our race and ethnicity.

God's fifth commandment to Moses in the Book of Exodus, chapter 20, verse 12, to honour our fathers and mothers is to honour our ancestors and heritage: our ethnicity and race. We do so to live long in the lands that God has given us: our countries.

With Christianity, self-respect should come. God created us in His image.

Whether our countries re-engage with our Christian heritage depends largely, although not entirely, upon whether our churches do. Mending the West mends Western Christianity.

That requires us to recognise there is Western Christianity. It is Western. It is Christianity.

If churches are to contribute to mending our countries instead of contributing to our decline, our churches need again to be Christian. They need again to be ours. A mended Church of England would be English. A mended Church of Scotland would be Scottish. They would be comfortable being so.

To practice Christianity is to defend it, for us and our race. Western Christianity fares best in Eastern Europe because the West fares best in Eastern Europe.

Christianity fares best outside the West. No longer can we afford to take Christianity to the world as we did through our Age of Empires. We need to revive Christianity at home.

In 1921, English-born composer Gustav Holst and poet Sir Cecil Spring Rice created the patriotic hymn 'I Vow to Thee, My Country.' In a diocese newsletter in August 2004, the Bishop of Hulme claimed the hymn was heretical. By 2020 at St Andrew's Anglican Church, Roseville, the hymn had become 'I Vow to Thee, My Saviour.'

Patriotism and nationalism are Scriptural because love and tribalism are. The Bible is a book of tribes, races, and nations, defending city-states with walls.

God created tribalism. He discriminates.

People created globalism and individualism. They are the heresies.

If Western Christianity is to survive, our churches must again vow to Thee, my Country. My parish church did, Remembrance Sunday 2024.

Western churches do not really vow to Thee, my Saviour. Churches often include images of worshippers, but in September 2021, the Washington National Cathedral announced that it would replace windows featuring Christian Confederate generals Robert E. Lee and Thomas Jackson with windows advocating for black people. It would overlay stone tablets venerating Christian Confederate soldiers with a stone tablet by a black poetess.

This was not a cathedral for worshipping God. It was a cathedral for worshipping black people.

At best, Western churches disregard Western people and religion: Christianity. At worst they push us aside.

They prioritise other races for church roles. They welcome immigrants with no regard for the will of God or the impact upon their countries, ethnicity, and cultures, including Christianity. Colonial European churches laud not God but indigenous peoples and their religions. Preferring other races to their race makes Western churches feel holy, when they no longer are.

People can be sinful without being broken, but our churches remain broken. Until we deal with being broken, we cannot deal with sin.

Not to attend church is to forgo opportunities for connectedness, culture, and correcting a church. Mindlessly giving offertory or other support to churches neglecting Scripture is lazy.

Centring people with free will and choice, Christianity rejects totalitarianism. The critical analysis we apply to the pronouncements of other human authorities we should apply to preaching from ecclesiastical authorities.

Among the facts against which to measure clerical teaching is the Word of God. Instead of imputing to God what we want God to say, reason is to read Scripture.

Ignorance, stupidity, and naivety are not Biblical. Knowledge, reason, and pragmatism are.

God created reality. He created biology and nature. Christianity produced the scientific method.

In chapter 2, verses 14 and 15 of his Epistle to the Romans, the Apostle Paul suggested that non-Christians acting *"by nature"* according to God's moral laws *"show that the requirements of the law are written on their hearts."* That is to say, morality is natural.

Like Saul of Tarsus, Western Christianity needs a Damascene conversion. God need not inspire any modern-day Paul to write more Scripture. Churches need only to read and preach the Scripture already here.

Scripture has not changed for almost two thousand years. God has not changed. Human nature has not changed.

The West has changed, since each world war. Translations of

Scripture have changed.

Like everything else, translations of Scripture should seek the truth, in this case the word and will of God. Translations preferring people's will are fraud.

Any church that presumes to reform or replace Scripture needs reforming or replacing itself. During the Reformation in sixteenth-century Europe, Luther believed the Roman Catholic Church had forsaken Scripture. The Pope excommunicated him. Feeling that the Church in Rome did not represent them and their cultures, several central, western, and northern European ethnicities formed Protestant churches.

Today, many Western churches no longer represent Western people and cultures. So destructive have many become, if saving Western countries requires us to lose them all, we should. Western Christianity requires it.

Ending our Age of Ideology would sweep ideological churches away. They are slipping away anyway.

Luther did not want new churches to form. He wanted the Church in Rome to reform.

We would be better served by a Second Reformation reforming Western churches to serve God and thus represent Western people and cultures again, than by letting those churches disappear with the rest of the West. If we want God again to smile upon us, we must again smile upon Him.

If Western churches decide to save themselves, they can return to Christianity and their founders. Western Civilisation came to include Christianity. If Western churches want to save Western Christianity, they would do well to defend Western Civilisation.

Western churches can care at least as much about us as they care about everyone else. Like other human authorities having neglected us for decades, that will not happen in an instant. There is no more trust from us in Western churches than there has been trust by Western churches in God of late.

Christians will not mend our race and ethnicities by prayer alone. Prayer is not a substitute for action.

Western Christians weakly trust God to do a lot of things, like arrest the decline of Western Christianity, but when it comes to helping other races, we speak and act. All we need to do is apply the time and effort we apply to helping people of other races to helping people of our race.

God gave our forebears the means to build and defend our countries and cultures. He saw fit to give us the same means.

To secret ourselves away in prayer without acting on those means is slothful. It is an insult to God. God aids us on mortal earth through us: his adjuncts in action.

He expects us to punish people who harm us and thwart people threatening to harm us, not embrace them. Psalm 109 is a prayer for vengeance.

When Western churches again side with the West rather than against us, ours will be churches again. When we stand again for Scripture, embracing what God embraces and rejecting what He rejects, we will be Christian again. We will give people a reason to be Christian.

We are not the saviours of the world; Christ is that. Sacrificing us saves no one.

Christians of other races aid their race. If they aid our race, it is incidental to them aiding their race, or themselves.

They remain rational, moral, and faithful. We need again to be like Christians of other races.

19. PRAGMATISM AND COMPASSION

People are all subject in some degree to their environments. Before the Great War, ours were cultures of service and duty, especially among the wealthy, able to afford them.

Compassion is kindness and generosity of deed. It is not sympathy, empathy, or morality, although it normally accompanies them. Compassion is cognitive and practical. It can be noblesse oblige.

The richest passenger aboard the Royal Mail steamship *Titanic* before she sank in 1912 was American businessman John Jacob Astor IV. Forty-seven years of age, Astor gave up his place in a lifeboat to save two frightened children.

Since the Great War and especially since World War II, our environment has changed for the worse. If the majestic *Titanic* sinking on her maiden voyage was a metaphor for our glory, hubris, and misadventure headed into the Great War, then the loss of the tiny submersible *Titan* in 2023 while travelling to the undersea wreck of the *Titanic* was a metaphor for our smallness, hubris, and brokenness a century later.

The *Titan* owner's chief executive was Stockton Rush. "By the time we're done testing it," Rush told *Columbia Broadcasting System News* in 2017, referring to his submersible *Cyclops*, "I believe it's pretty much invulnerable."

The interviewer pointed out that people said "pretty much" the same about the *Titanic*, before she sank.

"That's right," responded Rush, "and I will go all out and put my money where my mouth is." Money cannot buy everything.

The *Cyclops* was a precursor to the *Titan*, originally called *Cyclops II*, launched in 2018. Rush dismissed his director of marine operations David Lochridge after Lochridge warned him that his submersible was unsafe.

In 2020, Florida maritime instrument manufacturer Teledyne Marine published an interview with Rush, in which Rush said that he did not want to employ fifty-year-old white men because they were not inspirational. Rush would presumably not have found John Jacob Astor IV inspirational.

Lochridge, like Rush, was white. He turned forty-eight years of age in 2020. Rush turned fifty-eight. Our compassion for our compatriots had waned with our increasing individualism.

"I have broken some rules to make this," Rush boasted to Mexican film-maker Alan Estrada in 2021.

Calling something *Titan* does not make it Titan. Rush and four passengers died when the submersible imploded in June, 2023.

However un-inspirational Rush might have found middle-aged white men, a lot of them, like Lochridge, were very good at what they did. Flying up rather than sinking down, Icarus would have been a better name for Rush and his submersible.

Pragmatism is being practical: reality and reason. It is dealing with the world as it is, rather than presuming our countries remain as they used to be or trusting our dreamy visions of the world we want it to be.

The Islamic and Pashtun nationalist Taliban regime in Afghanistan aided al-Qaeda in its terrorist attacks on America in September 2001, killing three thousand Americans. In response, America attacked and defeated the Taliban.

Unwilling to defer to racial and cultural differences, America and other Western countries set about creating the Afghanistan we wanted countries to be. Through the ensuing twenty years of war and occupation, America expended two to three trillion dollars aiding Afghanistan, instead of aiding America. Thousands of Western troops died.

In August 2021, assuming she had created a new Afghanistan, America withdrew her troops. Within days, the American-trained Afghan army crumbled. The Taliban resumed control of the country.

All the time and money we devote to education and other propaganda cannot make people of other races into the people we want them to be. They do not become what we want them to be in their countries or in ours. Nor do their children.

Cultures might change over time and generations, especially in new environments. They might not. People decide.

Mark Leach was born to an irreligious Jewish mother, making him Jewish, and an irreligious Roman Catholic father. As a teenager in South Africa, he became a Christian. He later became an

Anglican Church reverend, still commemorating Passover. Conversing with me at a function in the Killara Hotel in November 2023, Mark said our biggest problem was what he called the atomising of people.

I called it individualism. Mark nodded.

That was the first time I heard of atomising people. Two nights later, Friday night, I heard of it a second time.

The New South Wales parliamentary secretary for multiculturalism Mark Buttigieg, born to immigrants from Malta, addressed a Diwali event in Chatswood. Contrary to Mark Leach, Mark Buttigieg spoke of the need for the atomisation of people.

Buttigieg presumed that atomising people would mean we see only humanity. It does not. It means we see only atomic selves and only our atomic selves at that.

Plainly the scores of Indians, Chinese, and other immigrants in the audience that Friday night did not atomise people. The dance, music, decorations, and food were proudly Indian. "Happy Diwali," people greeted each other. There was no "Happy Holidays" as we of the West said in place of "Merry Christmas." The New South Wales parliamentary website included among Buttigieg's interests political philosophy.

Blasphemy is not an offence against Christians. It is an offence against God.

God's feelings might be cause to dictate what people say and do. Our feelings are not.

When we were societies, we sought to accommodate each other's' views held widely enough, notwithstanding that we disagreed with them. We compromised.

Among the contentious issues we explored pragmatically was abortion. In Australia, opponents of abortion and advocates of abortion rights compromised by prohibiting abortion except when the pregnancy endangered the woman's life, but letting each woman decide whether her pregnancy endangered her life.

There is no inalienable right to life. Foetuses often die naturally, quite apart from anything that women do. Nature is pragmatic.

Ceasing to be societies, we ceased accommodating each other's views. Abortion advocates ran roughshod over opponents' sensitivities to allow unrestricted abortion rights, at least through the first part of a pregnancy. Conversely, abortion opponents in America ran roughshod over the needs of people wanting access to abortion.

Before American president Ronald Reagan ended rational consideration of abortion in America in the 1980s, there was a line of thought, especially among Protestants, that life began at birth. Thus abortion was not murder and not immoral. Abortion was not good, but nor was it bad.

If life begins at any point between conception and birth, then abortion before that point is not murder. When life begins is arguably a matter of science. At the least, it has regard to the knowledge that the scientific method brings. It is also arguably a matter of philosophy, determined by rational thought. It became a matter of ideology, determined by decree.

The issue of abortion is Scripturally uncertain enough for Christians not to be consumed by it. Chapter 5, verses 11 to 31 of the Book of Numbers set out a test to determine whether a wife has been unfaithful. It involves administering a potion such that, if the wife has been unfaithful, she suffers.

The meaning and implication of the passage are unclear. If the wife's suffering is a miscarriage, as some commentators believe, then the unborn child dies because of the mother's sin: her adultery. Presumably, but not certainly, the child was conceived by her adulterous affair. For the Bible to condone administering a potion to kill an unborn child is to condone abortion, at least in cases of adultery.

Other commentators believe the adulterous wife suffers barrenness or other distress. If so, then no passage in the Bible condones abortion.

Conversely, no passage in the Bible condemns abortion. Chapter 25, verse 23 of the Book of Genesis recognises that the patriarch Isaac's wife Rebekah's pregnancy produced in time two nations. Chapter 5, verse 1 of the Book of Jeremiah talks of God consecrating the prophet Jeremiah before he was born. The two verses speak to specific unborn, the lives they came to lead, and the roles God gave them. Neither passage denotes the ordinary unborn a person.

Chapter 1, verses 39 to 45 of the Gospel of Luke describe a visit by Jesus' mother Mary to John the Baptist's mother Elizabeth, while the two women were pregnant with those future figures. At verse 44, Elizabeth speaks of feeling her unborn baby leap in her womb knowing that the unborn Jesus within Mary is nearby. The events venerate motherhood, but whether they demonstrate that life begins at conception is problematic.

This was John the Baptist in the presence of Jesus. Elizabeth's feeling foretells the adult John recognising Jesus as the Son of God. The passage might have no relevance to the ordinary unborn. Neither of those two foetuses was going to die naturally.

Furthermore, the text describes Elizabeth's feeling. The unborn John might not have felt a thing. He might not have leapt at all.

For a mother to feel such joy from her baby within her is a wonderful thing. It does not imply that the baby feels such joy. When a mother feels no joy in the unborn child she carries, as she might for any number of reasons including conception by rape, there seems less relevance than ever for the text.

Treating an unborn child as human life is cause to punish a person who harms a pregnant woman and so kills her unborn child as a murderer. Chapter 21, verses 22 to 25 of the Book of Exodus say as much.

Morality arises within tribes: people connected in a common identity with a common good. A moral objection to abortion, if there is one, is on behalf of the tribe and the unborn child, that child being a child of the tribe. Any moral obligation of a pregnant woman not to have an abortion is no less than the reciprocal moral obligation of the father and his family and clan, as well as the rest of their shared tribespeople, to provide for the mother and her baby.

There are no mutual moral obligations without tribal connections. There are no reciprocal moral obligations with people from another ethnicity or race. There should be no moral objections to aborting mixed-race babies.

A common good does not mean childbearing for its own sake. It means producing people providing for the common good.

For the good of the woman and her family, there should be no moral objections to aborting babies conceived through incest, with its genetic complications, or with Down syndrome or other conditions preventing the eventual adults from keeping themselves. A woman might even feel a moral obligation to abort a child becoming a lifelong encumbrance upon her tribespeople.

That is a matter for her to decide. If her tribespeople believe they can compel her to carry her baby through to birth, then they also have a moral obligation to keep that child thereafter.

If aborting babies for biological reasons sounds like eugenics, then that should not make us condemn abortion. It should make us consider eugenics, rationally as always.

Of necessity, morality is pragmatic: promoting what in fact aids tribespeople rather than what people think aids them. Any course, action, or omission that harms tribespeople is immoral, however much anyone means well. Outcomes matter.

Any moral condemnation is for people to enforce among their own, for their family, ethnic, and racial good. Christians and everybody else have no moral interest prohibiting abortions among people of other races.

Zealotry can reflect brokenness, when the zealotry is to our detriment. Middle-class white Christians enjoying their contraception do well to worry more about their families, race, and culture, including Christianity, than about poor black women having abortions. Those black women can make their own decisions free from the sanctimonious dictates of white people with no obligation to keep them or their babies.

Compassion for people unable to support themselves should mean we want birth control for them. We should want them to have abortions. Leaving another race struggling to support itself so we can indulge our white people's burden to aid and regulate that race is selfish.

Primarily a Western trait, compassion can also be a Jewish trait. The Jewish religious duty of *tzedakah* provides charity to people of other races, which Gittin 61a of the Talmud sees as a means of making and keeping peace. It has not worked for Israel.

Aiding people and animals, compassion does not require connectedness. Compassion does not require reciprocity.

Western compassion for people of other races became incredibly resilient after the Holocaust. It persists in the face of abuse, exploitation, and brutality, as it rarely before did.

Calling upon our countries to aid people of other races knowing we personally remain unaffected demonstrates our individualism. Compassion for people of other races at our compatriots' expense is immoral.

Compassion ought to be moral. It ought to be rational.

The Gaîté Lyrique theatre in Paris occupied the elegant façade of the nineteenth-century Théâtre de la Gaîté. In December 2024, the theatre gave two hundred African immigrants free tickets to a

Reinventing the Welcome for Refugees in France conference.

After the conference, the immigrants refused to leave, forcing the theatre to cancel performances and cease operating. Through the ensuing weeks and months, the number of immigrants occupying the theatre swelled to more than four hundred, with drug dealing and violence.

"They've invited them into the theatre," remarked Great Britain News television presenter Leo Kearse in February 2025, "and what they've done is sort of created an immersive theatre experience of modern Europe." Staff abandoned the theatre at the end of February, 2025.

"I think it's okay," commented one younger visitor, in March 2025. "It's just diversity."

Police evicted the immigrants in mid-March 2025. In May 2025, the re-opened theatre warned that it was near bankruptcy.

Trust in some people is rational. In other people, trust is irrational, when fear can be rational. Dread moves people to be careful.

The Snowden family was a prominent family in the American south. Young black Travis Lewis lived with his parents on a property in the Snowden estate on Horseshoe Lake, Arkansas. In September 1996, Lewis murdered Sally Snowden McKay and her nephew Joseph "Lee" Baker in their family mansion.

Sally's kind-hearted daughter Martha McKay forgave Lewis for the murders. Believing in the power of forgiveness to better people, Martha aided Lewis's release from prison on parole in 2018. She employed him as a groundskeeper, giving him a home in her historic mansion. In March 2020, he stole ten thousand dollars from her, she dismissed him, and he murdered her too.

Concepts like compassion to all sounded lovely in theory. Concepts failing in practice, threatening to harm us or people for whom we care, we should abandon.

In October 2024, the Park Inn at Walsall, near Birmingham, housed asylum seekers. "The hotel was a way of her giving to a wider community," her sister Alex said later of English mother Rhiannon Whyte, working there aged twenty-seven. "Rhiannon never understood how scary the world really could be."

After Rhiannon finished her shift one evening, Sudanese asylum seeker Deng Majek followed her. At a nearby railway station, he stabbed Rhiannon twenty-three times with a crosshead screwdriver, killing her.

20. POLITICAL PHILOSOPHIES

Schools of thought rise and fall. Ideas spread and recede.

Through the twentieth century, particular political and economic philosophies came to matter more than they should. They became ideologies. Ideologies mattered more than they should.

Political and economic philosophies manifest in a range of systems and policies, affecting different people differently. Rationality and irrationality, morality and immorality, lie in their detail and circumstances.

People matter more than systems. The only systems that rational people uncritically reject are those pointed against them or God.

Instead of an unwavering devotion to any particular system or hostility to any other, reason wants whatever system to whatever degree and in whatever form best suits a particular people, place, and time. No system might be completely, universally, and eternally right or wrong.

People differ. Places differ.

Times differ. What is best can change.

The only necessity is a common nationalism or other tribalism. Morality depends on it.

Tribalism is not a philosophy. It is nature.

If aspects of different philosophies serve us, then we might want all those aspects. We might want a hybrid of systems, treating different issues differently, to whatever degree and in whatever form suits.

Countries already have hybrid systems. If socialism is government intervention in economic activity, then from much of Europe, Sweden looks socialist. From Britain, much of continental Europe looks socialist. From America, Britain and Canada look socialist. From free-wheeling and dealing frenetic Hong Kong, America looks socialist, in economic terms.

Politically, our optimum outcome might well be classic

liberalism. It might not be for other races.

People promote and protest policies and politicians with labels without there being clear and consistent senses of what those labels entail. What is mainstream or moderate to one person is dangerous or extreme to another.

Being denoted progressive, conservative, or liberal is immaterial, as is political left or right, far left or far right. Political left or right in one time or place is often the other in another time or place, as is progressive, liberal, and conservative. The differences in times can be brief and distances between places short.

Many policies do not fall easily into one category or another. Different people categorise policies differently. People often categorise contradictory policies together.

Policies denoted progressive do not progress. Those denoted conservative do not conserve.

Policies denoted liberal have become illiberal. Following the Holocaust, an ideological liberalism increasingly replaced classic liberalism.

One person's liberty should not come at another person's expense. One person's right should not be another person's imposition.

If the political far left and traditional far right seem much alike, it might be because different political spectra cut across each other. Liberty versus authoritarianism, even totalitarianism, is a spectrum.

Losing their biological connectedness after a second world war and the Holocaust, rich young white people rebelled against their parents. Repeating that each generation, the Western rich progressed from being politically right to being politically left.

The political right remained focused upon making rich people richer. The political left became the rich.

For much of the twentieth century, the political left and right were ideological. Centrist politics was avowedly pragmatic: concerned only with whatever functioned best for people.

With the collapse of Soviet communism in 1989 and 1991, the West submitted to the right about money and the left about people. What had been centrist slowly became right-wing extremism, for refusing to submit to ideology.

The primary political spectrum became ideology versus reason. For its commitment to reason, free speech, and independent thought, classic liberalism became far right, as it had never before been.

Everybody wants to ban something. Different people want to ban different things. They each accuse their opponents of the same bigotries, idiocies, and phobias of which their opponents accuse them.

The political left progressed from redressing real economic inequity suffered by poor white people to redressing the ideologically decreed inequity that students learnt at university and college. The left progressed from protesting against governments and big corporations to operating their human resources departments.

Rich and powerful people might laugh. Poor and powerless people do not.

Australian prime minister from 1975 until 1983, Malcolm Fraser was right wing for his disregard of Australian workers. He became left wing for his devotion to other races.

Enriching themselves still further, rich white people proudly aid other races. No longer aiding poor white people, the political left sneers at them. It went from wanting to improve Western Civilisation to bringing it down.

Western nationalism and racism used to be left wing, for protecting poor white people. They became far right when everything defending white people did.

Thus people of other races but ours are rarely far right. At worst, we label them socially conservative. The cultural traditions, religious devotion, and sexual morality we do not tolerate among conservative white people we respect among other races.

Outside the West, it is all very different. Political divisions mean less than they mean in the West.

Racism, nationalism, and other tribalism unite people, all be they different people. Political and economic systems all remain racist, nationalist, and otherwise tribal because people remain connected. They retain their ethnic and racial self-respect.

Even communism encompasses a range of policies in theory and inevitable practice. Chinese communism failed through its ideological period and Cultural Revolution. It prospered after Mao Zedong's death in 1976, becoming pragmatic, overtly nationalistic, and a hybrid system. Always politically nationalistic, Chinese communism became culturally nationalistic too.

In East Asia, businesses co-operate with governments for their national good. The Chinese Communist Party, through the Chinese state, operates a collective capitalism. If China was Western and we were willing to look through the language of communism, we could call China fascist.

Abandoning ideology enabled China's rise. So did ideology consuming the West.

We feed factories in other people's countries, creating the Chinese Empire. We sell our countries for thirty pieces of silver, or for brown paper cups of steaming black coffee.

In 2020, images from China reached social media forecasting Chinese rule of America before the end of the century. America's fingertip soldiers at their telephone touchscreens vowed it would never happen, but it was not up to them.

No powerful people seemed to mind. Treason has no meaning without nationalism.

In an address to the World Internet Conference in September 2021, South African-born billionaire Elon Musk lauded China. Making ever more money, he would continue increasing his investments there.

Musk might have thought he need not worry about China. His Space Exploration Technologies Corporation, formed in 2002, planned the colonisation of Mars.

By February 2024, Musk should have worried. *Business Insider* news reported China's plans to crush him.

The problem with freedom is giving people the freedom to harm us. Liberties are luxuries for people connected in a common nationalism.

With nationalism, predatory businesses prey upon other races. Without nationalism, predatory businesses prey upon their race. It's closer.

Without a common nationalism, free markets are immoral because people are immoral. Governments need to regulate businesses and their managers, but governments are also immoral.

Authorities can be beneficial, but to safeguard their compatriots, even to think of having compatriots, requires a common nationalism. They might see something righteous in benefiting other races while neglecting their own, but it is right for other races.

Western Civilisation includes democracy. When we enjoyed classic liberal democracy, our governments served us. Without a common nationalism, we have come to serve our governments.

Representative democracy has become nominal. Elected officials only represent, or say they represent, the people electing them to the extent they must to win re-election. Elections become just another process of appointment.

Democracy assumes that electors are correctly and fully informed about candidates regarding the issues upon which voters determine their votes. There is no democracy when electors are deceived, but without a common nationalism and so morality, electors become vulnerable to lies, manipulation, and deceit from candidates and their advocates.

Western democracy died when our governments began acting wilfully against our wishes and interests, in furtherance of other races or not. We never voted for our decline. We never voted away our inheritances.

Collective decision-making presumes the wisdom of many exceeds the wisdom of one. For participants to possess and feel confident in a collective decision, however they voted, they need common interests.

Seeing governments' disengagement from them, people are similarly disengaged from governments. Without representing people, democracy becomes no better than dictatorship.

Indeed, people fare better under dictatorships defending and asserting their interests than under democracies that do not. People's only demands of their dictators are that their dictators agree with them.

While we see only our individual interests, other races enjoy collective interests too. Western countries host immigrant councils like the Muslim Council of Britain, established in 1994, with which the British government consults.

Colonial European countries also host indigenous races' councils. In 2023, forty percent of Australians voted in favour of establishing a permanent elected body reserved for indigenous Australians, to make representations to parliament and the government of the day on any matter it wished.

Indigenous Australians would have retained their general parliamentary and government representation. While other Australians had only one representative body, indigenous Australians would have had two, had the second body proceeded.

Respecting other races' collective interests, we could consider our collective interests too. We used to.

We need only debate and decide what candidates, political parties, and policies best aid us and our cultural, economic, and other ethnic interests. Our representatives could then co-operate.

Representatives of other races co-operate with their own regarding issues affecting their race. We without nationalism tear each other apart.

Voters do not vote in gratitude. They vote for the future.

Immigrants stop voting for us when they can vote for candidates of their race, provided those candidates reflect their interests as those interests seem to them to be. We vote for them too. If democracy does not represent their interests, and they have the power to introduce a system that does, they can vote democracy out of existence.

Behind political and economic systems stands the same racial reality standing behind everything else. Multicultural capitalism flows from rich white people's disinterest in the well-being of other white people, without thought of the merits of their race and ethnicity making them rich in the first place, along with races' general disinterest in the well-being of races other than their own. Multicultural socialism redistributes wealth racially, also without thought of merit.

In November 2025, New York City elected democratic socialist Zohran Mamdani mayor. Before winning the Democratic Party primary in June 2025, the Ugandan-born Indian published a policy document *Stop the Squeeze on NYC Homeowners*. Mamdani declared he would "*Shift the tax burden from overtaxed homeowners in the outer boroughs to more expensive homes in richer and whiter neighborhoods.*"

Mamdani probably had a point, given the city's property tax system, but immigrant races are not as socialist with their wealth as they are with ours. The 2022 American Community Survey reported that Indians had the highest median household income of any ethnicity in America.

Immigrants prevail over the ethnicity that inherited and built a country when the latter votes one way but voters from all races vote another way. Democracy amidst racial or religious diversity empowers races or religions to disenfranchise others. Diversity and democracy don't mix.

For democracy to safeguard a race's destiny regarding issues affecting different races differently, the ballot boxes must be theirs.

Europeans that founded and built Rhodesia and South Africa reserved for themselves majorities of their parliamentary seats until 1979 and 1994 respectively, temporarily retaining their racial self-determination.

Retaining their racial self-determination, Fijians reserved a majority of Fiji's parliamentary seats from 1992 until 2013, when they were again securely in the majority. Democracy by race is pragmatic democracy.

Democracy withstands diversity regarding issues similarly affecting every race. In the 2024 American presidential election, voters from all races felt aggrieved by financial pressures, illegal immigration, and gender ideology. Prosecutors not prosecuting other alleged wrongdoers having prosecuted Donald Trump, voters feeling persecuted sided with him.

Our problem since the Holocaust has been that fascism espoused nationalism. When critics accuse us defending our inheritances of being fascist, they force us into silence or other submission rather than be accused of being fascists, but democracy and every other political system bar one before World War II was nationalistic.

Only Soviet communism denied people their ethnicities, countries, and cultures. After Nazi Germany and the Soviet Union signed a non-aggression pact in 1939, communists supported Nazism, until Germany invaded the Soviet Union in 1941.

Philosophies don't kill people. People kill people.

Under threat in war, Russians quickly recovered their racial connectedness. Nationalism strengthened them.

Nazism was an abbreviation for National Socialism, sharing capitalist wealth among all Germans. Letting national socialism define nationalism is like letting national socialism define socialism.

People insisting prejudice is never justified are prejudiced against nationalists. It is our nationa-phobia, in the language of ideology. We fear nationalism in our World War II frame of mind because Jews and we fear Nazism.

Jews had no racial reason to fear other fascism, until Nazi Germany brought fascist Italy to heel in 1938. Freemasons and communists have special reason to fear fascism. For most of us, every reason to fear fascism is reason to fear any totalitarianism.

Totalitarianism characterised communism, Nazism, and Italian fascism, although any political system can be totalitarian. Western democracies are becoming totalitarian, but not with democracy or with being Western.

Like Soviet communism and China during the Cultural Revolution, Western democracies are becoming ideologically totalitarian. In April 2025, the *Times* newspaper reported British police arresting thirty people a day for computer communications allegedly *"offensive,"* causing *"annoyance"*, *"inconvenience,"* or *"anxiety,"* and so forth, under various British laws.

In October 2025, following an anonymous complaint, Police Scotland investigated Claire Mackie-Brown for telling a Scottish television interviewer she was "born and bred here." Police found *"no evidence of criminality."*

Later in October 2025, the Metropolitan Police, Scotland Yard, announced that it would cease investigating *"non-crime hate incidents."* It would continue recording them.

"Gender binary was a key feature of the Nazi racist policies," claimed a Police Scotland internal document in May 2025. When authorities accuse dissidents engaged with biological reality or expressing sexual morality of being Nazis or neo-Nazis, they may well intimidate those dissidents into abandoning reason and morality. They also redefine Nazism.

They give people cause to see Nazism as rational and moral. Thus they imply that other political philosophies are irrational and immoral.

In fact, all countries accepted biological reality until the early twenty-first century. All recognised sexual morality until the late twentieth century.

In November 2025, the Reform U.K. party leader posted to social media an emblem marked family, community, and country. The chairman of Britain's Conservative Party equated it to a Nazi badge.

Labelling the safeguarding of Western families, communities, and countries as fascist, Nazi, or neo-Nazi makes fascism and Nazism attractive. Governments outside the West safeguard theirs. Our governments used to safeguard ours.

In spite of communists worldwide having killed tens of millions of people since 1917, during the 1983 Australian election campaign, future prime minister Bob Hawke mocked Australians' fears of communists: reds under the bed. Hawke said Australians could not hide their money from his future government under their beds because the communists were there.

We could just as readily mock Western fears of fascists: black shirts under the bed. It seems like everything Western is allegedly fascist.

Defending our families, ethnicities, and inheritances as people of other races defend theirs is not fascism. It is equality.

It is connectedness and collective self-respect. It is nationalism.

To be pro-German is to be anti-Nazi, as Nazism unfolded. To be pro-Russian is to be anti-communist, as Soviet communism operated.

A century before totalitarianism was Bonapartism. Napoleon was nationalistic, militaristic, and authoritarian.

Crises can necessitate temporary authoritarianism. During World War II, Britain suspended general elections. The government curtailed British liberties for the war effort.

We might not need to fear authoritarianism, provided we share the same nationalism. Nationalistic authoritarianism might be our only means of saving us from totalitarianism of any type.

As a practical matter, we sometimes need something unsavoury in the interim to carry us from where we are to where we want to be. Behaving unsavourily might be our only path to progress to the ideal.

In a close three-way election and without any candidate achieving a majority vote, socialist Salvador Allende became Chilean president in 1970. By 1973, amidst Allende's clashes with congress and the judiciary and with fear of communism rife, many Chileans believed Allende's presidency to be ruining Chile. General Augusto Pinochet removed Allende from power in a bloody coup.

By 1988, the threat of communism in Chile had passed. Pinochet submitted himself to a referendum on his rule, promising to give up power if he lost.

Pinochet lost. He gave up power. Democracy resumed.

Authoritarianism among other races might or might not suit us. Whether it suits those other races is a matter for them.

There is no point debating political and economic philosophies in abstract while we fade into oblivion. People need any means remaining, if only temporarily, for defending themselves and their ways of life.

We respect that for other races. We no longer respect it for us, but any system that saves and aids a people is better than any system that does not.

21. REVOLUTION

If people and animals must fight and kill to survive, they normally do. We used to.

Like us, Turks suffered the Great War. Like us, East Asians suffered World War II. They all recovered, continuing to defend and assert their ethnicities, cultures, and countries.

Their losses in war inspired them to treasure their ethnicities, cultures, and countries more. Our losses through two world wars should have led us to treasure ours more too, but in the natural, perennial struggle to survive, we stopped struggling.

Every other race but ours would fight its ruination, but much of the broken West no longer cares. The rest has largely given up.

Even many of us wealthy feel helpless to affect the actions of our authorities. If we do not indulge ourselves and everybody else, we plod along not doing anything significant.

However much we hoped that some elections and referenda would help, our landed and moneyed aristocracies keep getting what they want. Britain was not reborn by exiting the European Union in 2020. We just ceased being bits of Europe. Britain's open borders with continental Europe became our open borders with the world.

Powerful people do as they want to do. In Western countries, they might consider themselves globalist. They are irredeemably individualist.

The few Western leaders claiming to defend their people's interests generally do little. Much like our other leaders, they prefer parties with aperitifs.

It is not enough for them to fight the people we would fight. They need to fight for us. A ballroom doesn't help.

We would not have allowed our undoing before the Holocaust. We fought for our people and countries, for better or for worse, ironically defending our governments who in time abandoned us.

In April 1862, during the American Civil War, the Union army's major general of volunteers was Ulysses S. Grant. Following the bloody battle at Shiloh, critics called for Grant's removal. "I can't spare this man," answered president Abraham Lincoln. "He fights."

Lincoln appointed Grant general-in-chief in March 1864. Grant went onto lead the Union army to victory.

In time, the Union healed relations with the Confederacy's heirs. The Holocaust ruptured America's wounds again.

The Great War ravaged Europe. The imposition of ideology depended upon war.

Most of the West retained enough self-belief to refuse the ideologues, until World War II allowed the Soviet Union to impose communism on Eastern Europe. Ideologues gained in zeal, while the Western rest lost our last will to resist. The imposition of individualist ideologies was more gradual than the imposition of Soviet communism had been.

Following the momentary mob, people talk of being on the right side of history, but history does not end until time ends. Beliefs, behaviours, and attitudes change. They change again.

However appealing an idea Soviet communism seemed to some after the diabolical Great War, it proved a moral and cultural failure. It also proved a political and economic failure, although not for the people in charge.

Through their Soviet subjugation, East Europeans and Soviet citizens seemed lost, but beneath their occupation and oppression, ordinary people remained true to themselves. While communist authorities lied, parents taught their children the truth. Parents taught their children their cultural heritage.

We could do the same with our children. Beneath the deception, we remain Western. Englishmen and women remain English, and so forth.

In their resistance, East Europeans and Soviet citizens persevered, finally freeing themselves from ideology in 1989 and 1991. People who lost their countries, cultures, and ethnicities to communism after each of the world wars recovered them.

Soviet communism ended not just for the resistance of ordinary people, but for powerful people losing something of their communist conviction. Mikhail Gorbachev, the eighth and final leader of the Soviet Union, recognised the failings of communism. He embarked upon reform. Gorbachev ceased enforcing communism on Eastern Europe. He relaxed it in the Soviet Union.

Gorbachev believed Soviet communism could be reformed to work. It could not.

Neither can individualism. Nothing defying human nature can be reformed to work.

Like Soviet communism after suffering the First diabolical World War, letting go of our countries, cultures, and ethnicities seemed a good idea after suffering a Second diabolical World War. We imagined there being no more wars or holocausts, at least in Europe.

We were wrong. War is no less normal than peace.

Also like Soviet communism, individualism has proven to be a moral and social failure. It has been a political and economic failure for ordinary Europeans and colonial Europeans, if not yet for people in charge.

Westerners bitter with their life's course might vent their anger at Western Civilisation. That is scapegoating. Their malevolence will not exhaust until they direct their malevolence to where reason directs their malevolence should be: the people or policies responsible for their ills.

Perhaps they should be angry at their governments, big businesses, or universities. Perhaps they should be angry at news and entertainment media.

Perhaps they should be angry at anyone espousing individualism, with its isolation and immorality. Quick to see people as victims of oppression where there is none, we fail to see the most widespread victims of all: the victims of ideology, including us.

The "government of the people, by the people, for the people" that Lincoln lauded at Gettysburg in 1863 was nationalist representative democracy, but nationalism commands that we safeguard our compatriots, as they safeguard us. The Civil War ravaged the American South, spurring gun manufacturing and contributing to American gun culture and the Wild West mythology.

To enforce a claim that people are our compatriots by killing them was tragically irrational in the American Civil War. It was tragically irrational in Ukraine in 2022.

Russians and Ukrainians both suffered under Soviet communism. Following the collapse of the Soviet Union in 1991, their nationalist leaders shared their pains of the past and tried to craft co-operation for the future. The two Slavic ethnicities shared a common race and much of their cultures.

There is no international law akin to national law. There are treaties and the like between nations, voluntarily entered and voluntarily maintained.

Contracts between countries last only as long as both countries want. In 1994, Russia guaranteed Ukrainian security, for which Ukraine transferred her nuclear weaponry to Russia. Two decades later, Vladimir Putin's Russia reneged, invading Crimea in 2014.

A fair and free referendum in Crimea in 2014 might have returned Crimea from Ukraine to Russia. Referenda not fair and free are pointless.

Given their commonalities and connectedness, a nationalist Russian leader would have supported Ukrainian nationalists within pan-Slavic, pan-European, or pan-Western nationalism. Instead, Russian president Putin consigned Russians and Ukrainians to their deaths by ordering a full-scale invasion of Ukraine in February 2022.

Putin demonstrated his individualism, not nationalism. He valued neither Russian nor Ukrainian lives.

Julian Lennon had long said he would not sing his father John's song 'Imagine', before singing it in April 2022 to protest the Russian invasion. The song praised a world without countries, but Ukrainians fought and died to keep their country.

Countries mean borders. Peace needs borders. I wondered whether people thought about the words of songs they sang or to which they listened.

The defence of Ukraine was not a defence of democracy. It was nationalism: Ukrainian nationalism. Ukrainians valued their country, culture, and ethnicity.

We valued theirs too. Western governments defended Ukrainians as they no longer defended other European ethnicities, threatening to fight fellow-European Russians as they no longer fought other races.

When others deny us peace and security, fighting and dying is better than simply dying. Better still is fighting and winning.

Like Ukrainians, we too need not accept changes ruining us. Fortunately, we need not yet fight for our families and ethnicities in war.

There are no humanitarian wars. There are only wars.

When people fight and kill, our only interests should be ours. We might assist our friends and allies, like Ukraine, but not races contemptuous of us.

We should not send our troops to die defending them. We are not the world's policemen. We tried that through our days of Empire, for which we now hate ourselves. Fighting other people's wars has gone very badly for us.

Defending a country requires people believing they have a country. It requires nationalism. Why would we fight for our compatriots no longer considering us compatriots?

Nor should we fight for our governments. They have long stopped fighting for us.

Why would we die for our countries our governments are giving away? If our governments want us defending our countries, then our governments need to defend them. Otherwise, defending our countries begins with replacing our governments.

No less in nation states than in primitive tribes, the moral legitimacy of human authorities depends on them being connected with the people they rule. Without moral legitimacy, there is only force and manipulation.

National law depends upon nationalism, connecting lawmakers, law interpreters, and law enforcers with the people over whom they make, interpret, and enforce the law. The common law and an independent judiciary presume a common nationalism. Without it, judicial perspectives of justice have become personal, sectional, or alien.

In July 2025, in violation of planning laws, Britain's Home Office housed asylum seekers at the Bell Hotel in Epping, Essex. Eight days after arriving in England by boat, Hadush Kebatu, an Ethiopian aged at least thirty-eight, sexually assaulted a fourteen-year-old English girl and later an Englishwoman, among his five crimes over two days.

Epping Forest District Council sought asylum for Britons from the asylum seekers, but London's Court of Appeal in August 2025 and Britain's High Court in November 2025 held that British law prioritised asylum seekers' rights. By November end, Clearsprings Ready Homes had acquired eight homes for the Home Office to house more asylum seekers in Epping.

Queen Elizabeth II was the last legitimacy of Britain's failed ruling class. Her funeral in September 2022 was the first state funeral in Britain since that for Winston Churchill in 1965.

Of Churchill, we mourned one man. Of Her Late Majesty, we mourned Britain, the West, and Western Christianity, without saying so and perhaps without realising so. They were obvious at her funeral as they were normally not by 2022. Her Late Majesty had been proud of Britain and her history. She had been steadfast in her faith.

Her passing was the passing of service and duty. They had given way to rights and entitlement.

Largely inept in 1914, rulers around the West became increasingly more inept thereafter. Once they might have cared about being inept. They ceased seeming to care. They had other priorities.

They brought us the Great War. They kept us there.

They brought us World War II in Europe. They made us vulnerable to World War II in Asia, Australasia, and the Pacific Ocean.

They brought us mass interracial immigration. While we mourned Her Late Majesty in 2022, Indians and Pakistanis fought each other in Leicester.

Preferring instead the ambience of private clubs and luxury boats, our rich closed our factories in which they no longer set foot. They see economic news being good or bad for governments, businesses, and them, rather than for people struggling to get by.

They lead our churches away from Christianity. They manage the news and entertainment media willing to deceive. They oversee our universities prepared to let the West dissolve.

Many of our rich do not like ordinary people. They do not like the look of them, even those ordinary people tending to their air-conditioning units or dish-washing machines. They have no interest in ordinary lives, livelihoods, or viewpoints, expecting ordinary white folk to accept our unnecessary decline.

They might not particularly like other rich people. They might not particularly like anyone.

Indifferent or even hostile to their race, cultures, and countries, they submit us to other races, cultures, and countries. Altogether unperturbed if the rest of their race disappeared, they might be comfortably relieved.

Their agents might not be rich, but are richer than many of their compatriots. Not only are rich and powerful people to blame.

Their weak and faithless followers are at fault.

The contempt of powerful white people for powerless white people invites the same contempt in return. Born of that worsening cruel neglect, ordinary people have developed a deep distrust towards authorities.

Rational people are confident only in people with competence. They trust only people with integrity.

Spreading nonsensical conspiracy theories does not reflect problems with the people. It reflects problems with authorities.

Authorities have become untrustworthy. Accustomed to the ludicrousness of their deceit, people believe more ludicrousness.

Exacerbating that mistrust, authorities call cases against them conspiracy theories. A sentiment widely acknowledged among people who delight in it, they call a paranoid conspiracy theory in people who object.

Until 1989, East Europeans looked westward for support. Today, Westerners realising our plight look to Eastern Europe.

People who suffered Soviet communism recognise the falsity and cruelty of rule by ideology. Again representing their ethnicities, East European authorities defend their countries and cultures, not just from Putin. They defend the West, often from us.

Ideologies rejecting Western Civilisation or all civilisations might have originated among irreligious Jews and the disillusioned of our own. They became the status quo of a suicidal West.

Westerners feel rebellious because they rail against their forebears, families, and race, but they mouth every dictate presented to them. They are not rebels. They are sheep, buying and believing as others direct.

Rebellion fights the living, not the dead. Rebellion fights new norms, not old norms. Rebellion fights the status quo.

Rebellion fights the rich and powerful, not the poor and powerless, even when it counts some of the rich and powerful among the rebels. Rich, powerful, and other influential people normally drive revolutions and reform.

Today, to be truly rebellious among most Western ethnicities is to be like people of other races. It is to appreciate being of our ethnicities and race. It is to honour our forebears, defend our relatives and compatriots, and safeguard our descendants.

It is to be human. It is to be normal.

Weaning unsuspecting people from ideologies that are all they know is difficult, even with shocks like the wars that brought ideologies upon us. Realising their beliefs about themselves and their role in the world are falsehoods imposed upon them since their infancy is disconcerting. The end of communism in Eastern Europe in 1989 and the Soviet Union in 1991 frightened people accustomed to their constraints, while dissidents celebrated their release.

Overcoming communist ideology in Eastern Europe required perseverance over decades. Overcoming other ideologies requires perseverance too. The depth of penetration of individualist ideologies across the West by 2025 far exceeds that by Soviet communism in Eastern Europe and the Soviet Union through the twentieth century.

Ideology is an industry. The end of ideology can be an industry too.

Aiding our compatriots can replace aiding everyone else. Pride can be in our people. Reality and reason can be our catch cry, as can human nature.

The changes need not all come at once. They need not be every change here contemplated and there may be other changes. They need only allow us again to think, feel, and act as nature would have us: as people of other races do.

If we cannot persuade, we need to prevail. If we cannot break the nexus between the ideologues and their ideologies, we need to break the nexus between the ideologues and influence.

Without other advocates, to whom do poor and powerless people turn but the revolutionaries and radicals? When those who would ruin a people also rule them, people must revolt. The only useful power is power over the powerful.

We should not fear revolution. We should fear a lack of revolution.

Better than revolution are the rich and powerful fearing revolution. The people best placed to preserve our inheritances for our descendants were the people best placed to bring us to our knees. Reform by our rich and powerful would be the most peaceful and efficient.

There is no comparable position in the West today to the general secretary of the Communist Party of the Soviet Union, when Gorbachev took the role in 1985. The West fragments power.

Our Age of Ideology would soon end if enough influential white people calmly re-engaged with reality, returned to reason, and again respected human nature. They would then reconnect with their ethnicities, recover their racial self-belief, repossess their cultures, and set about repossessing their countries.

Some people of other races recognise the benefits we bring them, even if others among their race do not. Those people lack the power to free us, without us wanting to free us too. Mending us is up to us.

Mending our ethnicities requires people caring for our ethnicities to co-operate. Co-operation among compatriots is nationalism. Co-operation across connected ethnicities is pan-nationalism, ultimately for us Westernism.

A biologically reconnected, rationally self-respectful, and culturally replenished West could be better than we have ever before been, with our new technologies and having learnt from all that we have seen. We could be content, happy, and secure, as we were before the Great War, perhaps again getting a little better every year.

It is not too late to save our families, ethnicities, and race. It will simply become more difficult the longer we take to start. People once gone cannot return.

SELECTED BIBLIOGRAPHY

Bita, Natasha, 'Hamas massacre 'was anti-racist', says Monash University researcher,' *The Australian* newspaper, 9 February 2025.

Black, Jeremy, *Imperial Legacies: The British Empire around the world*, Encounter Books, New York, 2019.

Bovill, James and Tanya Gupta, 'Rhiannon felt safe working at asylum hotel, her death will haunt us forever,' *British Broadcasting Corporation News*, 24 October 2025.

Browne, Thomas, *Pseudodoxia Epidemica: or, Enquiries into very many received tenents, and commonly presumed truths*, Edward Dod, London, 1646.

Burke, Edmund, *Reflections on the Revolution in France*, James Dodsley, London, 1790.

Churchill, Winston, 'Zionism versus Bolshevism: A Struggle for the Soul of the Jewish People,' *Illustrated Sunday Herald* newspaper, 8 February 1920.

Copernicus, Nicolaus, *De revolutionibus orbium coelestium: On the Revolutions of the Heavenly Spheres*, Johannes Petreius, Nuremberg, 1543.

da Vinci, Leonardo, *Thoughts on Art and Life*, translated by Maurice Baring, English edition, American Embassy, London, 1906.

Dawson, Tyler, 'Book burning at Ontario francophone schools as 'gesture of reconciliation' denounced,' *National Post* newspaper, 7 September 2021.

Devlin, Kate, 'Tory row erupts over jibe comparing Reform logo to Nazi badge, *Independent* newspaper, 24 November 2025.

Einstein, Albert (author) and Ze'ev Rosenkranz (editor), *The Travel Diaries of Albert Einstein: The Far East, Palestine, and Spain, 1922–1923*, Princeton University Press, Princeton and Oxford, 2018.

Gay, Peter, *Freud: A Life for Our Time*, W. W. Norton & Company, New York, 1998, page 448.

Guthrie, Dan, 'The English countryside still feels like a white middle-class club. We can – and will – change this,' *The Guardian* newspaper, 1 March 2023.

Herzl, Theodor, *Der Judenstaat: Versuch einer modernen Lösung der Judenfrage (The Jewish State: Proposal of a modern solution for the Jewish question)*, Verlags-Buchhandlung, Vienna, 1896. Translation by Sylvie d'Avigdor, Nutt, London, 1896, later revised by Scopus Publishing Company, New York, 1943.

London, Oli, *Gender Madness: One Man's Devastating Struggle with Woke Ideology and His Battle to Protect Children*, Skyhorse Publishing, New York, 2023.

Lopez, Linette, 'China's E.V. takeover: Inside Beijing's grand plan to dominate the future of electric cars,' *Business Insider*, 25 February 2024.

Luther, Martin, *Von den Jüden und ihren lügen (On the Jews and Their Lies)*, Hans Lufft, Wittenberg, 1543.

Marx, Karl and Friedrich Engels, *Die Deutsche Ideologie (The German Ideology)*, Marx–Engels–Lenin Institute, Moscow, 1932.

Orwell, George, *Nineteen Eighty-Four*, Secker & Warburg, London, 1949.

Paine, Thomas, *The Age of Reason; Being an Investigation of True and Fabulous Theology*, Barrois, Paris, 1794, 1795, and 1807.

Pearce, Georgia, "An experience of modern Europe!' Leo Kearse blasts Paris theatre managers facing bankruptcy after opening doors to migrants,' *Great Britain News*, 28 February 2025. Georgia Pearce, "I wouldn't shop here – would you?' Paris visitors hit out as migrants take over theatre and spark financial turmoil – 'I'm speechless!',' *Great Britain News*, 11 March 2025.

Phipps, Alison, *Me, Not You: The Trouble with Mainstream Feminism*, Manchester University Press, 2020. Melanie Newman, Julie Bindel, and Hayley Dixon, 'Oxfam training guide blames 'privileged white women' over root causes of sexual violence', *The Telegraph* newspaper, 9 June 2021. Danyal Hussain and Rory Tingle, 'The message seems to be a woman who reports rape is a contemptible white feminist': Outrage at Oxfam staff training document blaming 'privileged white women' over root causes of sexual violence,' *Daily Mail* newspaper, 10 June 2021.

Scruton, Roger, *Gentle Regrets: Thoughts from a Life*, Continuum, London, 2006.

Shipley, David, 'Epping is being punished by the asylum system', *Spectator* magazine, 27 November 2025.

Trotsky, Leon, *History of the Russian Revolution*, Germany, 1930, translated from Russian by Max Eastman, Simon & Schuster, New York, 1932.

von Treitschke, Heinrich, '*Die Juden sind unser Unglück*' ('*The Jews are Our Misfortune*'), *Preußische Jahrbücher (Prussian Yearbooks)*, 15 November 1879, also published in a pamphlet *Ein Wort über unser Judenthum (A Word About Our Jews)*, 1880 and 1881.

FURTHER READING

Carlson, Susan, *The Art of Diversity: A Chronicle of Advancing the University of California Faculty through Efforts in Diversity, Equity, and Inclusion, 2010–2022*, University of California, Oakland, 2024.

Steven Brint, 'The U.C.'s Corner-Office Revolutionary,' *Quillette* magazine, 9 April 2024.

Fang, Lee, 'San Francisco's progressive racism,' *UnHerd*, 12 October 2024.

Fox, Mira, 'How the anti-sex scene backlash has its roots in antisemitism, *Forward* news, 16 February 2023, regarding the Hays Code enforced until 1968.

Füredi, Frank, *The War Against the Past: Why The West Must Fight For Its History*, Polity Press, Cambridge, 2024.

Silva, Angelica, 'For some South Asian women in interracial relationships, lying to parents is a necessary step to being happy,' *Australian Broadcasting Corporation News*, 18 February 2024.

Subramanya, Rupa, 'Report: D.E.I. Is Transforming the National Science Foundation,' *The Free Press*, 10 October, 2024.

ABOUT THE AUTHOR

Simon Lennon has travelled throughout Europe, America, Australasia, Asia, and the South Pacific, seeing how similar European peoples are to each other (wherever we live) and how different we of the West are to everyone else. He has university bachelor's degrees in science and law and university master's degrees in commerce and business. He is married with six children.

His non-fiction collection *The West* comprises the following sixteen books:

Mending the West
The Unnatural West: An Overview
The Tribeless West: An Overview
The Homeless West: An Overview
The Vanishing West: An Overview

Individualism
Western Individualism
The End of Natural Selection
The Need for Nations

Identity
People's Identity: Race and Racism
Of Whom We're Born: Race and Family
Biological Us: Gender and Sexuality

Nationalism
A Land to Belong: Nationalism
The Failure of Multiculturalism

Cultures
Reclaiming Western Cultures
Christendom Lost
Aiding Islam

He is also the author of another non-fiction book, two collections of short stories, and five novels.

www.ingramcontent.com/pod-product-compliance
Lightning Source LLC
Chambersburg PA
CBHW021619270326
41931CB00008B/771